Test Prep Series

MW01154799

Book 2

GRE®

Analytical Writing: Solutions To The Real Essay Topics

60 Solved Issue and Argument topics to stir-up your brain for creative ideas

Expert Strategies and simplified methods to produce focused responses

Scoring Guides for Issue and Argument tasks as per the revised GRE Guidelines

VIBRANT
PUBLISHERS

GRE® Analytical Writing:
Solutions to the Real Essay Topics - Book 2

ISBN-10: 1-946383-29-5
ISBN-13: 978-1-946383-29-7
Library of Congress Control Number: 2014900726

Table of Contents

Dear Student,

Thank you for purchasing **GRE Analytical Writing: Solutions to the Real Essay Topics - Book 2**. We are committed to publishing books that are content-rich, concise and approachable enabling more students to read and make the fullest use of them. We hope this book provides the most enriching learning experience as you prepare for your **GRE** exam.

Should you have any questions or suggestions, feel free to email us at **reachus@vibrantpublishers.com**

Thanks again for your purchase. Good luck for your GRE!

- Vibrant Publishers Team

1

Introduction to the Analytical Writing Measure

The Analytical Writing Measure is intended to assess your ability to think critically and write effectively about a topic while following specific directions. You will not need any specific content knowledge to complete either in this portion of the test. The purpose of both writing pieces is to determine your readiness to perform appropriately at the graduate level.

During this portion of the test, you will complete two writing tasks: Analyze an Issue and Analyze an Argument. For each portion, you will have 30 minutes to read the prompt and directions and to plan and execute your response.

The two tasks are opposite in their nature. During the Analyze an Issue task, you will write persuasively as you express your point of view on the selected topic, which may be in the form of an opinion, a recommendation, a claim and reason, or the presentation of two points of view. It is important to read the directions carefully to insure that your response is addressing the prompt correctly and to enable you to receive the highest score.

During the Analyze an Argument task, you will evaluate an argument to determine the strength of the facts and assumptions that it presents. You may be asked to evaluate the evidence in order to determine if the assumptions are correct, formulate questions that will need to be answered before determining if the assumptions are correct, what further evidence is necessary before the argument can be declared correct, or what steps should be completed before accepting a recommended course of action. As in the Analyze and Issue task, in the Analyze an Argument task, reading and following the directions carefully is the best way to insure that you receive a high score for your efforts.

This page is intentionally left blank.

2

Analyze an Issue Task

As you complete this task, you will have an opportunity to express your point of view on an issue. Because it is essentially your opinion, there is no "correct" answer. You must, however, support your point of view with sufficient evidence to show the strength of your argument. You may agree completely with the statement about the issue, partially agree with it, or completely disagree with it. Be certain to stay on topic and follow the directions carefully.

For example, you might be presented with a statement similar to the following: It is always best to look before you leap. You should understand this statement to mean that you should consider the consequences before taking any action. The directions may instruct you to write a response in which you discuss the extent to which you agree or disagree with the statement and explain your reasoning for the position you take. If you agree with the statement, you should recall examples from your reading, your studies, or your own experience that support your position. Think about Holden Caulfield's actions in *The Catcher in the Rye*. His impulsive decision to spend some time alone in New York City before going home after his expulsion from Pencey Prep had unsatisfactory consequences. You may have taken some action in your own life that you regretted afterwards. On the other hand, you may disagree with the statement. Early explorers like Christopher Columbus had little idea about what they would find as they set out in their relatively small sailing vessels. If they had thought only about the dangers of their ventures, the new world would have been discovered much later. You can also take a qualified approach by agreeing with the statement to some extent. Remember, your approach is not important. The GRE essay readers are trained to evaluate a wide variety of approaches to the issue and evaluate them on their strengths and weaknesses and not on the opinion expressed.

The following is a comprehensive list of the instructions that will accompany the statements in the Analyze an Issue task.

a) Write a response in which you discuss the extent to which you agree or disagree with the statement and explain your reasoning for the position you take. In developing and supporting your position, you should consider ways in which the statement might or might not hold true and explain how these considerations shape your position.

b) Write a response in which you discuss the extent to which you agree or disagree with the recommendation and explain your reasoning for the position you take. In developing and supporting your position, describe specific circumstances in which adopting the recommendation would or would not be advantageous and explain how these examples shape your position.

c) Write a response in which you discuss the extent to which you agree or disagree with the claim. In developing and supporting your position, be sure to address the most compelling reasons and/or examples that could be used to challenge your position.

d) Write a response in which you discuss which view more closely aligns with your own position and explain your reasoning for the position you take. In developing and supporting your position, you should address both of the views presented.

e) Write a response in which you discuss the extent to which you agree or disagree with the claim and the reasons on which that claim is based.

f) Write a response in which you discuss your views on the policy and explain your reasoning for the position you take. In developing and supporting your position, you should consider the possible consequences of implementing the policy and explain how these consequences shape your position.

g) You may have had some experience with writing persuasively in high school or college, but you do not need to worry about specific rhetorical devices in order to complete this task and receive a high score. It is important to stay on topic, present your argument in a coherent and cohesive manner, and to recognize other points of view in order to strengthen your own. You should also make every attempt to use correct grammar, mechanics, and a variety of sentence structures to improve the fluency of your essay. The scoring guide that follows is reprinted from the Practice Book for the GRE Revised General Test, developed by Educational Testing Service.

Scoring Guide

Score 6

In addressing the specific task directions, a 6 response presents a cogent, well-articulated analysis of the issue and conveys meaning skillfully.

A typical response in this category:

a) articulates a clear and insightful position on the issue in accordance with the assigned task

b) develops the position fully with compelling reasons and/or persuasive examples

c) sustains a well-focused, well-organized analysis, connecting ideas logically

d) conveys ideas fluently and precisely, using effective vocabulary and sentence variety

e) demonstrates facility with the conventions of standard written English (i.e., grammar, usage and mechanics), but may have minor errors

Score 5

In addressing the specific task directions, a 5 response presents a generally thoughtful, well-developed analysis of the issue and conveys meaning clearly.

A typical response in this category:

a) presents a clear and well-considered position on the issue in accordance with the assigned task

b) develops the position with logically sound reasons and/or well-chosen examples

c) is focused and generally well organized, connecting ideas appropriately

d) conveys ideas clearly and well, using appropriate vocabulary and sentence variety

e) demonstrates facility with the conventions of standard written English but may have minor errors

Score 4

In addressing the specific task directions, a 4 response presents a competent analysis of the issue and conveys meaning with acceptable clarity.

A typical response in this category:

a) presents a clear position on the issue in accordance with the assigned task

b) develops the position with relevant reasons and/or examples

c) is adequately focused and organized

d) demonstrates sufficient control of language to express ideas with reasonable clarity

e) generally demonstrates control of the conventions of standard written English but may have some errors

Score 3

A three response demonstrates some competence in addressing the specific task directions, in analyzing the issue and in conveying meaning, but is obviously flawed.

A typical response in this category exhibits ONE OR MORE of the following characteristics:

a) is vague or limited in addressing the specific task directions and/or in presenting or developing a position on the issue

b) is weak in the use of relevant reasons or examples or relies largely on unsupported claims

c) is poorly focused and/or poorly organized

d) has problems in language and sentence structure that result in a lack of clarity

e) contains occasional major errors or frequent minor errors in grammar, usage or mechanics that can interfere with meaning

Score 2

A two response largely disregards the specific task directions and/or demonstrates serious weaknesses in analytical writing.

A typical response in this category exhibits ONE OR MORE of the following characteristics:

a) is unclear or seriously limited in addressing the specific task directions and/or in presenting or developing a position on the issue

b) provides few, if any, relevant reasons or examples in support of its claims

c) is unfocused and/or disorganized

d) has serious problems in language and sentence structure that frequently interfere with meaning

e) contains serious errors in grammar, usage or mechanics that frequently obscure meaning

Score 1

A one response demonstrates fundamental deficiencies in analytical writing.

A typical response in this category exhibits ONE OR MORE of the following characteristics:

a) provides little or no evidence of understanding the issue

b) provides little evidence of the ability to develop an organized response (i.e., is extremely disorganized and/or extremely brief)

c) has severe problems in language and sentence structure that persistently interfere with meaning

d) contains pervasive errors in grammar, usage or mechanics that result in incoherence

Score 0

A typical response in this category is off topic (i.e., provides no evidence of an attempt to respond to the assigned topic), is in a foreign language, merely copies the topic, consists of only keystroke characters or is illegible or nonverbal.

3

Solved Issue Tasks with Strategies

General Strategies

a) Restate the issue.

b) You could also determine what question is being answered by the statement. Creating a question may help you determine your position on the issue. If someone were to ask you this question, would you say yes, no, or maybe?

c) Next, create a statement that expresses the opposing viewpoint, using language similar to that of the original statement.

d) Think about alternative viewpoints. Is there another way to look at this issue? Can you qualify the original recommendation in some way? How can you answer all or some of the questions that you generated earlier?

e) Then, you must decide which point of view to address in your essay. Before you decide, carefully consider the following questions. You will have addressed several of them in the exercises you will perform below.

    i) What, precisely, is the central issue?

    ii) What precisely are the instructions asking me to do?

    iii) Do I agree with all or any part of the claim? Why or why not?

    iv) Does the claim make certain assumptions? If so, are they reasonable?

    v) Is the claim valid only under certain conditions? If so, what are they?

    vi) Do I need to explain how I interpret certain terms or concepts used in the claim?

    vii) If I take a certain position on the issue, what reasons support my position?

viii) What examples - either real or hypothetical - could I use to illustrate those reasons and advance my point of view? Which examples are most compelling?

f) Once you have decided on a position to defend, consider the perspectives of others who might not agree with your position. Ask yourself:

   i) What reasons might someone use to refute or undermine my position?

   ii) How should I acknowledge or defend against those views in my essay?

g) The next step should be listing the main reasons and support for your position. Keep in mind that the GRE readers scoring your response are not looking for a "right" answer—in fact, as far as they are concerned, there is no correct position to take. Instead, the readers are evaluating the skill with which you address the specific instructions and articulate and develop an argument to support your evaluation of the issue.

Issue Task 1

Governments should place few, if any, restrictions on scientific research and development.

Write a response in which you discuss the extent to which you agree or disagree with the recommendation and explain your reasoning for the position you take. In developing and supporting your position, describe specific circumstances in which adopting the recommendation would or would not be advantageous and explain how these examples shape your position.

Strategies

The best place to start your analysis is by breaking down the statement and identifying the inherent assumptions.

Statement breakdown

a) **Governments –** places the restrictions in the realm of the law

b) **Restrictions:** the nature and extent of the restrictions is unknown - this gives you a lot of room to explore – are the restrictions about scientific conduct? Do they include testing? How about work safety or waste management?

c) **Scientific research and development** – gives you the scope of the restriction

Assumptions

a) Governments have the responsibility of placing/lifting restrictions

b) Scientific research is bound by law

c) Restrictions on scientific research hinder progress

Once you have completed these steps, you need to write down the pro and con arguments, regardless of which position you take. Knowing the counterarguments (ideas in opposition to your own position) allows you to present a more rounded view of the subject, and gives you the opportunity of identifying contradicting evidence.

Pros and Cons

Pros

- More creativity
- More daring
- Reaching previously unexplored fields
- Faster research-development-production rate

- Less bound by current societal practices/notions of morality

Cons

- Ethics/crossing moral boundaries
- End justifies the means
- Untested products can find their way on the market
- Problems with work-safety
- Handling waste products and the environment
- Cruelty to animals/human experimentation
- Risk of science turning into business (profit over safety)
- Division of country based on beliefs (stem cell)

Examples

For a truly well rounded essay, examples are crucial. Here are some avenues that are potentially worth pursuing:

a) History is rife with examples – both the unethical human experimentation, and the great accidental discoveries (like penicillin) that greatly benefitted mankind.

b) The same goes for the news – scientific research that is testing the boundaries is always bound to attract controversy – think of stem cell research, cloning.

c) In this case, Science Fiction books and movies love showing the consequences of pushing the boundaries of science.

Lastly, spend a few minutes coming up with a roadmap. While at first it will slow you down, once you become adept at outlining, your writing speed will increase, and your essay will benefit from having a logical structure.

Sample Essay

Scientific research has always been tangled with the ethical dilemma of whether the end justifies the means. There is even an entire philosophical field called 'normative ethical theories' that is dedicated to examining standards for the rightness and wrongness of action and determining how an individual should act. In this case, while giving researchers a carte blanche allows science to explore uncharted territory and enables a faster research-development-production rate, it also opens the door to the horrors of unethical experimentation.

Even though studies have shown that animal research is neither necessary nor is it predictive for humans, animals still continue to be the most common subject of scientific experimentation. While the existing Animal Welfare Act offers reduced protection, removing all the restrictions on scientific research gives scientists a free pass to conduct experiments that would otherwise have been seen as animal cruelty, on the basis of inducing unnecessary pain. Furthermore, having no regulations when it comes to the species that can be used in experimentation, can lead to an increase in poaching when it comes to animals with rare properties or genetic similarities to humans. Like Thomas Edison said, "Until we stop harming all other living beings, we are still savages."

Unrestricted scientific research would not only impact the treatment of animals but also how human experimentation is conducted. The history books are fraught with examples of experiments that were often performed illegally, without the knowledge, consent, or informed consent of the test subjects. In the US for instance, the Cold War era brought about numerous psychological experiments for testing effective torture and interrogation techniques. There is even the famous case of the Holmesburg prison in Pennsylvania, where in the 60's and 70's, chemical experiments were performed on the prisoners who were injected with dioxin, a highly toxic compound. Perhaps the most telling and horrific example is that of the Nazi human experiments, from genetics to vivisections, poison studies and transplantation without anesthesia. What particularly draws attention to this case is not just the extent of human suffering, but also the justification used for the experiments: at the trial, several of the doctors argued in their defense that there was no international law regarding medical experimentation. This raises the question of how to judge abuses in regards to scientific experimentation without a body of law that governs the scientific practices.

Another issue also presents itself - no research restrictions means no regulation when it comes to testing. Take the example of the pharmaceutical industry - on the one hand, experimental treatments can find their way on the market much faster – on the other, pharmaceutical companies run the risk of becoming a business where profit supersedes safety. Current regulations require years of trials before drugs can be released for production – without them, companies can cut corners and push products on the market that can have serious untested side effects. Without government regulations, taking punitive action against companies that promote dangerous drugs to the market becomes difficult if not impossible, especially since, according to the law, they would not be committing any crimes.

Then there is the question of how to handle dangerous scientific research (viruses, chemical weapons etc.). Having no restrictions means people who are insufficiently prepared or have destructive agendas can get involved in potentially dangerous experiments. Researching subjects that would be better left alone and dealing with the consequences of pushing the boundaries of science are prominent themes of science fiction. Most post-apocalyptic scenarios of both books and movies come about from scientific experimentation – creating dangerous viruses that escape containment, like in The Stand, or opening up inter-dimensional portals to worlds of horror in Stephen Kings' The Mist.

Ultimately, no matter how seductive is the promise of freedom of research, rules and regulations has to be set in place to ensure that in the quest for knowledge we don't end sacrificing our own humanity. Existing restrictions have evolved based on our previous experiences with the potential horrors of unsanctioned experimentation, and they have been set in place to protect us – from ourselves.

Issue Task 2

> *Governments should offer college and university education free of charge to all students.*
>
> *Write a response in which you discuss the extent to which you agree or disagree with the statement and explain your reasoning for the position you take. In developing and supporting your position, you should consider ways in which the statement might or might not hold true and explain how these considerations shape your position.*

Strategies

A good starting point is to break down the statement and identify the assumptions it makes. Look for ambiguous phrasing and consider all possible exceptions – they represent weak points that you can defend or attack depending on your chosen position.

Statement breakdown

a) **Governments** – state funded education

b) **College and university** – does it include masters, PhDs?

c) **Free of charge** – what expenses are paid (tuition, board etc.)? How about following multiple studies simultaneously? What about existing scholarships and welfare packages?

d) **All students** – including exchange students?

All statements are based on a set of assumptions about the world and the way it works – many of these social norms are implicit due to subconscious associations. The basis of outlining assumptions is asking 'why': why should the government provide free education? Why should the education be free for all?

Assumptions

a) College and university education is desirable

b) Having more educated people is good for the state

c) The government has the resources to provide free university education

d) All students should benefit – including exchange students

Pros and Cons

Pros

- No more crippling debt (like seen in the US)
- An educated workforce is an economic imperative
- It is an investment in the country's own future (more students means more contributions)

- Bridges the gap between 'haves' and 'have-nots' – high tuitions can be a deterrent for brilliant students without financial means
- Compulsory education is already state funded
- Free education does not mean having lower standards – students still have to pass admission tests
- Stimulates the economy around universities based on the expected influx of students
- Educational excellence attracts talents from around the world
- Loyalty effect – talented people will not desert the country in search for better options
- Higher education is related to culture and civilization

Cons

- Existing programs already cover students that have financial issues (grants, scholarships, welfare etc.)
- It would be expensive – it would incur increased taxes or other trade offs
- System abuse – lingering or unsure students that waste taxpayers money on studies they won't complete
- No pressure to finish – a lowering of study quality (people can stretch out the education for as long as it takes, or put less effort into it)
- Exchange students will use the program and then return to their own countries (and contribute to society there)
- More graduates would dilute the value of a degree (a degree would become the norm, instead of a differentiating criteria
- Oversaturation of the job market (many graduates would be un or underemployed
- College degrees do not guarantee learning ability or job preparation

Examples

a) Look at nations across the globe, some have free university education (Denmark, Norway, Sweeden etc.), while others don't (USA, Romania, Germany etc.)

b) Percentages of employed university graduates

c) Economical contribution (pay grade and its relationship with graduation)

d) The relationship between literacy rate and economical power

e) Scientific and technological advancements

f) Tuition fees and debt

Sample Essay

Education plays an important part in everyone's life, it helps people overcome superstitions, keep in touch with the advancements of the world and gain a deeper understanding of how things function, instills respect, teaches people how to function and contribute to society while maintaining their own independence. Like Nelson Mandela said, 'education is the most powerful weapon which you can use to change the world."

Governments from across the globe have understood this crucial fact and acted in accordance by making education up to a certain level compulsory and free. Why should this government funding not extend to higher education as well? There is no doubt that promoting education is an investment in the future, like many studies have demonstrated by linking the literacy of a country with its economical growth. An educated workforce is an economic imperative - more students means more contributions, both in terms of finances and when it comes to scientific, technological and cultural advancements. Given the potential of a highly skilled workforce, some nations have already implemented policies that ensure free access to higher education for all students. In Sweden, attending university is free for all EU students. Denmark and Norway have similar policies. It is interesting to note that these countries have some of the highest living standards in the world and that their policies have been in place for several years with no major drawbacks to speak of.

On another note, state funded university education can also help bridge the gap between the haves' and 'have-nots'. High tuitions can be a deterrent for brilliant students without financial means – valuable talent can be lost to menial labor or even other countries, as students can leave in search of better opportunities. While most countries already have some scholarship programs set in place, they only cater to the extremely brilliant and promote a highly competitive environment. The students that fall just shy of the requirements have to contend with paying tuition, and in some countries, like the US, that lands them into crippling debt. Student loan debt in the US has made the front page of international newspapers with stories of ruined lives and people that have to dedicate a good portion of their life just to paying off the tuition fees. Having no debt means graduates have more buying power and can invest more in the economy.

Free university education can even have a direct effect on the micro-economy surrounding the campus based on the expected increase in the number of attending students. Like in the cases of Cambridge and Harvard, universities encourage the growth of towns next to campus sites – small businesses that cater to the students needs tend to flourish. An increase in the number of attending students can even have an effect on the construction market as dormitories get expanded to accumulate the intake of students.

Additionally, funding the student's education can have a loyalty effect - talented people will not desert the country in search for better options. It should also be noted that free education does not mean that there will be a drop in standards – students still have to pass admission tests, and pass their classes. This way, the system ensures that only the people that posses the necessary skills and determination to graduate can enroll. The Dutch system provides a good application of this principle – Dutch students get a loan from the government for their university tuition, and upon graduation, the loan is given as a gift. In essence, in the Netherlands, higher education is free – as long as the student graduates, which serves as a good motivation for people not to slack off or take on more studies than they can handle.

This goes to show that there are viable solutions for implementing free university education policies. Moreover, numerous countries have applied these policies with success for a considerable number of years. Given these practical examples and the potential benefits of a highly educated workforce, it would be a shame not to invest in our future.

Issue Task 3

In any field of inquiry, the beginner is more likely than the expert to make important contributions.

Write a response in which you discuss the extent to which you agree or disagree with the statement and explain your reasoning for the position you take. In developing and supporting your position, you should consider ways in which the statement might or might not hold true and explain how these considerations shape your position.

Strategies

A good starting point is to break down the statement and identify the assumptions it makes. Look for ambiguous phrasing and consider all possible exceptions – they represent weak points that you can defend or attack depending on your chosen position.

Statement breakdown

a) **Any field** – is it applicable to all fields? How about highly complex ones that require specialized knowledge?

b) **Beginner –** how do you classify the beginner? Based on age? Experience? Knowledge?

c) **More likely** – does it refer to statistical probability (numbers game)? Does it refer to inherent qualities of the beginner?

d) **Important contributions** – what constitutes an important contribution? What is the classification criterion: applicability, usefulness, impact?

Assumptions

a) Beginners are more likely to contribute, since there are more beginners than experts

b) Important contributions are not based on experience

c) Beginners have more creative minds, while experts are set in their ways

Pros and Cons

Pros

- Thinking outside the box (integrating and reorganizing existing understandings – a process essential to beginners
- With age, cognitive abilities deteriorate, it becomes harder to process new information (experts are often older)
- Beginners are determined – they have something to prove
- Beginners are freer to experiment – experts are set in their ways

- There are greater numbers of beginners, so a larger chance to bring accidental contributions
- Beginners have more willingness to try or evaluate new paths
- Beginners have more time (experts are committed to multiple projects and often have to perform supervisory roles)
- Beginners have less to lose by pursuing risky avenues

Cons

- Beginners that make important contributions are considered experts
- The aging brain is similar to the creative brain (based on neural imaging) – low inhibitions, high scores on crystallized IQ
- Experts are more productive, have a better work ethic
- Some fields are very complex (entry level knowledge is insufficient to provide deep insight)
- For beginners, lack of practical application can lead to correct but irrelevant insight (researching avenues that lead to nowhere
- Focused research (knowing the field allows you to conduct a targeted research)
- Historically, most of the great inventions come from experts between the ages of 30 to 50
- Experts have more freedom of choice when it comes to the research topic (beginners are limited by supervisors
- Experts can get more funding, or obtain it easier than beginners can (reputation)
- Experts enjoy more credibility

Examples

a) Inventors and scientific contributors from the past

b) Studies linking age and creativity

c) Problem solving skills and methods (you can pair them up with the group that fits best)

d) Current research practices

Sample Essay

Humans have conquered their surroundings and overcome their limits in leaps and bounds marked by great innovations. Our ability to integrate and reorganize existing understandings, to bring new order to chaos, has been the driving force of our progress. It is no wonder that people seek to understand the process of innovation and encourage those that are most likely to succeed in revolutionizing the world.

So far, invention has been considered the patrimony of experts, and one of the reasons is the fact that, in order to be able to combine fragments of knowledge in new ways, one needs to have sufficient knowledge in the first place.

It is not difficult to understand why such perceptions abound, especially if we consider highly complex fields that require specialized, in depth, knowledge. Take for instance astrophysics or microbiology – a beginner in these fields would only possess summary knowledge of the forces at play and the processes involved. They wouldn't be able to revolutionize theories on dark matter without a basic understanding of quantum theories, and by the time they would have acquired this knowledge, they would be considered experts. This is also the case of Albert Einstein, whose major contributions in the field came as a steady progression after getting his PhD. Most important of all, Einstein's theory of relativity only started taking shape after years of teaching theoretical physics at the universities in Zurich and Prague, and two years spent studying continuum mechanics, the molecular theory of heat, and the problem of gravitation.

When it comes to establishing whether beginners or experts are more likely to revolutionize a new field, it is important to note that a lot of the past inventions have come from people that had to constantly struggle with a specific problem. A lot of the people that have contributed to the advancement of society were experts in a field (they were in the proper circumstances to encounter the problem, and possessed sufficient knowledge to recognize and solve the issue at hand). This is the case of prominent physician, John Snow, whose field work in tracing the 1854 cholera outbreak in London is regarded as the founding event of epidemiology. He encountered many cases of viral diseases as a physician, which, alongside his skepticism of the then dominant miasma theory of infection, spurred him on to research the Soho epidemic and discover the source of the outbreak.

Moreover, one should always keep in mind that it's not sufficient to have a good idea, a researcher should also be able to support it and make it known. This holds especially true when considering the basic conditions for any form of research to be considered a major contribution in a field. Namely, said research should revolutionize its field of study, it should be known by other experts in the discipline and obtain external validation (even if at a later point in time). In this sense, experts enjoy more credibility than beginners, and are likely to be taken more serious. Furthermore, experts already have networks in place and get quicker access to information like interesting research proposals and latest advancements. Companies and other researchers will choose to go to the person with a better reputation. The same can be said in terms of funding, experts can attract more funds for promising research– simply because they have more experience and an established reputation.

Studies have shown that experts are more productive and have better work ethic and time management skills. In addition, being an expert doesn't signify the death of creativity, like the statement implies, blindly sticking to one method has more to do with personality. The same goes for linking expertise with age, as neural imaging studies have shown that the aging brain is more creative, uninhibited and shows better crystallized IQ. Benjamin Jones has also found that over the past 100 years, the major scientific discoveries have come from people with ages between 30 and 50.

Overall, when it comes to having major contributions in a field, experts possess the advantage. They have more knowledge, an increased ability to organize the information they posses, more resources to fund research and a better work ethic than beginners.

Issue Task 4

The surest indicator of a great nation is represented not by the achievements of its rulers, artists, or scientists, but by the general welfare of its people.

Write a response in which you discuss the extent to which you agree or disagree with the statement and explain your reasoning for the position you take. In developing and supporting your position, you should consider ways in which the statement might or might not hold true and explain how these considerations shape your position.

NOTE: The above topic has wording similar to Issue Task 27 of GRE Analytical Writing Solutions to the Real Essay Topics - Book 1. However, if you read carefully you will notice that the task instructions are different. Hence, it is very important to read the topic as well as its instructions completely before you start to write your response.

Strategies

Statement breakdown

a) **Surest indicator** – Welfare is not the only indicator of greatness; it is not a causality relationship – welfare doesn't cause greatness, but can be used to measure it

b) **Great nation** – what constitutes a great nation? How do you define it? In terms of power, size, economy etc.?

c) **Rulers, artists or scientists** – categories of people whose contributions can be significant – are they the only ones with memorable achievements? What about athletes, spiritual leaders, military heroes, brilliant businessmen and other people that brought significant advancements in their fields?

d) **General welfare** - what is the degree of welfare? Meeting the basic needs of the people? What indicators do you use to measure it – safety, buying power etc.?

Assumptions

a) Great nations have a high level of welfare

b) The welfare of the people is more important than the achievements of rulers, artists and scientists

c) Rulers, artists and scientists are the only ones with notable contributions

Pros and Cons

Pros

- High living standards are a hallmark of civilized society
- Rulers, artists and scientists are not the only ones whose achievements contribute to a country's greatness
- Welfare is an indicator – something that when measured can tell the state of a country – it's economical and cultural prosperity

- Welfare encourages scientific development – in the sense that if people's basic needs are met, that gives them the freedom to pursue their vocations/ideals
- More programs and support systems for artists and scientists (scholarships, research funding etc.)
- Happiness studies are directly linked with productivity/ creativity
- People centered modern day philosophy – human resources are the most valuable
- Great thinkers (scientists) and artists are great in themselves, regardless of the nation they came from – their contributions transcend boundaries

Cons

- Historically speaking, countries are memorable due to the achievements of their rulers, artists and scientists
- Great rulers make welfare possible – they promote policies that support good living conditions for the citizens of the state
- Scientific advancements make life easier, increase the living standards
- Greatness is measured in contributions to world benefit – ruling principles like democracy, freedom of speech etc.
- Good rulers and scientific advancements drive the economy. Strong economies are indicative of great nations.
- A country's power is an indicative of greatness, and a major contributing factor in scientific advancements
- Cultural ideals help shape not only a nation, but the entire world

Examples

a) Civilizations of the past, to showcase what history considers to be great nations

b) Current great nations

c) Economical theories on welfare

d) Great achievements in the fields of science, great artists and commanders

Sample Essay

Current society, as a whole, has become highly invested in people centric policies – from governments that ensure the welfare of the citizens, to companies that place customer and employee values at their core. This transformation is in the spirit of Mahatma Gandhi's teachings, that "man becomes great exactly in the degree in which he works for the welfare of his fellow-men."

Throughout the ages, welfare has been an indicator of a nations' economical and cultural prosperity. High living standards point to economical stability, growth, abundance of resources – all of which are necessary to ensure that the populations' necessities are met. Moreover, the presence of welfare signals the existence of a cultural system capable of fostering the ideas necessary to support it. High living standards and civilization have always been linked – take for instance the great nations of the past, like Ancient Greece or Rome, hallmarks of civilization that have left a deep imprint on the world. In both of these cases, the quality of life of the average citizen was well above that of the people living in the neighboring countries – they had the buying power and the possibility to enjoy a wider variety of products and leisurely activities, while being less concerned with day to day survival.

In this sense, it can be said that welfare encourages creativity, by meeting people's basic needs which in turn gives them the freedom to pursue their vocations/ideals. Maslow's hierarchy of needs supports this idea. Maslow's theory states that an individuals' fundamental needs have to be fulfilled before he can focus on the higher level needs. What this means is that, for instance, metabolic requirements will tend to supersede self-actualizing actions, namely, artistic or creative activities will have to take a backseat to hunger or thirst. Countries where people's basic needs are being taken care of can afford to dedicate more time and resources to higher pursuits.

Moreover, countries with a high standard of living have the means to create programs and support systems for artists and scientists. The countries in northern Europe that are famous for the quality of life of the average citizen, have significant government support when it comes to education. Their tuition fees are much lower than in the USA, and they invest a greater deal of resources into scholarships and research funding than countries like India. More than that, the northern European countries strive to ensure not just the physical welfare of their citizens, but also their mental and ideological wellbeing by providing an open minded climate where diversity can thrive. As Plato postulated in the Republic, the stability and success of a political community depends on the moral character of the people who make up that community.

From these arguments, it becomes apparent that rulers, artists and scientists are not the only ones whose achievements contribute to a country's greatness. But rather, economical power, one of the main characteristics of a strong nation, is dependent on the consumers and their buying power.

Ultimately, when assessing a nation's greatness, it all comes down to what traits best represent it. From what we have seen so far, the welfare of a nation's citizens, closely tied to their economic power, provides a nurturing environment for talents that will end up shaping the rest of the world and contributing to the benefit of mankind. As such, it can be said that general welfare is one of the surest indicators of a country's greatness.

Issue Task 5

As we acquire more knowledge, things do not become more comprehensible, but more complex and mysterious.

Write a response in which you discuss the extent to which you agree or disagree with the statement and explain your reasoning for the position you take. In developing and supporting your position, you should consider ways in which the statement might or might not hold true and explain how these considerations shape your position.

Strategies

A good starting point is to break down the statement and identify the assumptions it makes. What is interesting to note in this particular case is the fact that the statement is counter intuitive: it seems to contradict common sense. The nature of the statement makes it suitable for philosophical and psychological arguments

Statement breakdown

a) **We** – general we of humanity

b) **Acquire more knowledge** – knowledge is cumulative – how to quantify it? Is it "true" knowledge? Is it "useful"?

c) **Things** – all encompassing term for the subject of knowledge; vague term: is it only specific things that become less understandable?

d) **Comprehensible** - understandable; how do you gauge a person's understanding? Based on how 'true' it is, or how much it conforms to current scientific trend?

e) **Complex and mysterious** – suggest awe in the face of the vastness of the universe; is it a feeling rather than fact based speculation?

Assumptions

a) The universe cannot be fully known – the sum of all knowledge cannot be attained

b) Discovering something always opens up new avenues of research

c) Knowledge is measurable – walking in the direction of "true knowledge"

d) We are not 'equipped' to be able to grasp all knowledge

Pros and Cons

Pros

- Knowledge is not linear – we also take steps back in our quest for truth
- What is 'true' now will end up being proved wrong in the future, as our understanding grows

- Knowledge is influenced by society/ dominating paradigms
- Each new question answered raises other questions
- More knowledge gained shows us just how complex things are (scientific models always grow in complexity)
- Our minds are not suitable for understanding the level of complexity of the universe
- We can only perceive what our senses tell us

Cons

- Knowledge is quantifiable
- knowledge is attainable, step by step (knowledge building)
- Not 'understanding" is a feeling – psychological effect
- Should not compare current knowledge with sum of all knowledge – but with how little we knew in the past (progress measured by how far we have come, not how far we still have to go)
- People feel overwhelmed by how much there is still to discover/ the vastness of the universe – it is a psychological effect (fallacy of insignificance)
- A fully known universe is boring – and that is frightening
- Average human intelligence has grown significantly
- High level, complex knowledge is attained by the brilliant and then parsed down
- We don't only accumulate information but also know how to process and understand it – we don't gather information for information's' sake

Examples

a) Scientific discoveries can prove how much we know or do not know about the universe

b) Psychology can show how our mind reacts to the universe, it's vastness, and how human minds are able to process knowledge and complex issues

c) Philosophy – the study of epistemology (understanding knowledge and how it is acquired)

d) Researchers – what do the foremost minds involved in the knowledge gathering process think about it

e) Biochemistry – abilities or limitations of the human mind

f) Books and movies that have explored the theme before

Lastly, spend a few minutes coming up with a roadmap. While at first it will slow you down, once you become adept at outlining, your writing speed will increase, and your essay will benefit from having a logical structure.

Sample Essay

The universe has always fascinated us – from the very dawn of civilization, when everything seemed shrouded in mystery and the unexplainable was the realms of the gods. The curiosity of the human nature is the driving force of our accelerated evolution and the reason why we have developed methods of systematic study – so that we are better able to understand and control our surroundings. As Sir Francis Bacon said - "knowledge is power".

At the heart of knowledge is the search for truth, and of the many ways people try to unravel the mysteries of the universe, scientific research is deemed to be a more accurate understanding of the world. That is because, in essence, scientific research is based on gathering observable and measurable evidence by formulating and testing hypothesis in reproducible experiments. Epistemology, the study of knowledge and how it is acquired, shows us that knowledge gathering is a cumulative process – new theories, no matter how revolutionary, have a basis in previous theories.

Saying that things become more complex and mysterious as we acquire more knowledge means operating under the false assumption that progress is measured by how much we have yet to discover. When humanity is at the start of the line, in terms of understanding the universe and its secrets, progress should be measured by how far we have come, not how far we still have to go. We should not compare our current knowledge with the sum of all knowledge, but rather with how little we knew in the past. Take, for instance, biology and how much we have progressed from believing that human sickness is a result in the imbalance of humors, to the current day advanced understanding of organs, tissues, cells – down to the DNA level. The same can be said for the rudimentary notions of geography of the past, namely the idea that the Earth was flat and that the Sun was orbiting around it. Comparing these notions to the current understanding of tectonics, landscape formation and astrophysics theories like the existence of dark mater, we can see how far our understanding of the universe has progressed, one step at a time. And while we can in no way say that we know everything that there is to know, we can certainly say that we are able to accomplish so much more than in the past, all thanks to a better understanding of our environment.

As such, the amount of knowledge the average individual possesses, has been steadily growing over the ages – the same can be said for our comprehension. What children learn and are able to grasp in schools today would have been part of the mystery of the universe in the past. This increase in knowledge was observed by Buckminster Fuller and named "the Knowledge Doubling Curve". He noticed that until 1900 human knowledge doubled approximately every century and by the end of World War II knowledge was doubling every 25 years. If one were able to travel through time to a period like the Middle Ages, our knowledge, technology, behaviors and speech would be seen as witchcraft. Like Arthur C. Clarke said: 'Magic's just science that we don't understand yet.'

Part of the issue of thinking that the universe becomes progressively incomprehensible is our wonder with the universe, which, while understandable, also inspires the idea that true knowledge is somehow unattainable. People feel overwhelmed by the vastness and complexity of the universe and hold the belief that our simple mind cannot comprehend it - this psychological phenomenon is called the fallacy of insignificance. Colin Wilson in The Stature of Man claims that this fallacy is an effect of modern day society that conditions individuals to lack self-worth, as a mechanism of ensuring compliance – people want to become part of the system, in order to escape their feelings on unimportance. People end up operating on the idea that as an individual, they do not matter much in the grand scheme of things, which is why they should belong to something greater, that gives their existence meaning.

Last, but not least, people want to believe that the universe maintains its shroud of mystery because the idea of attaining full, complete knowledge is frightening – a fully known universe is predictable and boring, like professor Farnsworth from Futurama stipulates: : "And, now that I've found all the answers, I realize that what I was living for were the questions!"

Issue Task 6

To understand the most important characteristics of a society, one must study its major cities.

Write a response in which you discuss the extent to which you agree or disagree with the statement and explain your reasoning for the position you take. In developing and supporting your position, you should consider ways in which the statement might or might not hold true and explain how these considerations shape your position.

Strategies

Restate the issue, perhaps by reversing the order of the sentence components.

In other words:

Studying a society's major cities leads to understanding its most important characteristics.

Determine what question is being answered by the statement. This will help you begin to think how you would answer it and whether or not you agree with the original statement.

How can one understand the most important characteristics of a society?

Parts of the original statement that provide evidence that you can affirm or refute.

a) **understand** - This implies more than identifying or listing. Understanding occurs at a deeper level.

b) **most important** - The superlative -most- implies a selection process that eliminates less important characteristics. What process and how was it created?

c) **society** - this can refer to any social entity, large or small.

d) **major cities** - Major might refer to size of population, state capitals, centers of industry, number of educational institutions. How were cities identified as major?

e) **study** - This implies a deep examination. What aspects of these cities should one study to gain understanding of society's most important characteristics?

Next, create a statement that expresses the opposing viewpoint, using language similar to that of the original statement.

Opposing viewpoint:

Studying its major cities is not a means to understanding a society's most important characteristics.

Identify the parts of the opposing statement that provide evidence to refute or affirm. In this case, the evidence is the same as that in the original statement except for the word not.

a) **not** - In this case, it removes studying major cities as a means of understanding society's most important characteristics. Using this statement forces the writer to develop other means of understanding societal characteristics.

Alternatives

Is there any other way to look at this issue? Can you qualify the original statement in some way? Is it possible to partially agree with the statement?

New viewpoint:

To understand the most important characteristics of a society, one must study its major cities as well as small towns and rural communities.

Identify the parts of the new statement that provide evidence to affirm or refute.

a) **one component** - This suggests that studying major cities does not illuminate all of a society's most important characteristics.

The following essay uses this balanced position. In other words, both major cities and smaller towns or rural areas have qualities that make them repositories of a society's important characteristics. List some examples to use as support. Because the issue does not mention what the important characteristics of a society are, you will have the freedom to suggest what they might be.

Examples:

Diversity - Cities are the likely repositories of this characteristic. Small towns are more homogeneous.

Culture - Major cities provide greater access to cultural events and displays, e.g., theater, symphony, museums.

Education - Access to a wide range of educational institutions exists in major cities.

Self-reliance - Lack of a variety of products and services makes residents of small towns more self-reliant.

Sample Essay

To claim that one can understand a society's most important characteristics by studying only its major cities ignores all of the other social structures that exist within a country. A country as vast as the United States, for example, is made up of fifty states that act as independent entities in many respects. Within each of those states reside groups of citizens united or divided by race, ethnicity, religion, or social class. Some states do not even have what may be considered a major city. To presu.me that only major cities are worthy of study minimizes the contribution of smaller constructs to the characteristics of the larger society. On the other hand, many large cities are composed of smaller societies that may represent those that exist in the remote and far-flung areas of this large country.

Before determining where examples of a country's most important characteristics reside, one would need to identify what those characteristics are. If diversity is near the top of the list, then major cities would be the places to study it. New York City is home to neighborhoods like Little Italy, Chinatown, Spanish Harlem, and Hell's Kitchen. Additionally, residents of NYC live in neighborhoods that cater to lifestyle or economic class, such as Greenwich Village, SoHo, and Park Avenue. Small towns in rural America tend towards homogeneity, and their residents have little exposure to racial or ethnic diversity.

An appreciation for fine arts might rank high in importance as a societal characteristic, and, once again, cities are home to myriad institutions where the fine arts are displayed or performed. Only in major cities is one likely to find museums of art, symphonies, opera houses, and theaters for the live performance of plays and musicals. Residents of small towns may only have a high school band and access works of art on the Internet, thus limiting their exposure to and appreciation of the fine arts.

Physical access to institutions of higher learning elevates the citizens of a society and is universally considered to be important. Graduates of small town high schools must generally leave home to obtain a college degree, whereas students in a major city need travel only a few blocks to attend an Ivy League college, a state university, a design institute, or a school for the performing arts. Lack of access may even discourage children in remote areas from attending college, reducing the overall level of education in those towns and making them less desirable to study for identifying the important characteristics of society.

In contrast, small cities and rural towns may be better locations to study characteristics that are as important as the ones cited above. Residents of these communities are more likely to combine their efforts to support a member in need. One cannot miss the donation cans on convenience store counters that are used for collecting money to help a family that has lost everything to a fire or has a child undergoing expensive medical treatment. The local grocer has a community bulletin board where service clubs can post upcoming events to raise funds to send the high school baseball team to Florida for spring training or to build new dugouts at the town's playground. If concern for one's neighbors ranks high on the list of important characteristics, then small towns are suitable subjects of study.

Residents of rural towns retain some level of self-sufficiency, although the expansion of the Internet has had some impact on that quality. Vegetable gardens are common, and housewives still can and freeze their yields for future consumption. Husbands are jacks-of-all-trades. They mow their own lawns, paint their own houses, and use their own tools to repair broken machines or change a washer on a faucet. Kids on farms have chores as well as school work to complete each day. An important characteristic of any society might be hard work combined with ingenuity, and small towns are likely to be populated with people who display this.

On the whole, the original statement has veracity. Major cities are microcosms; their residents are representative of the society as a whole. Visitors to those cities can see people from all walks of life who are from varied backgrounds and display talents and abilities that one may find isolated in smaller towns. Cities are growing while small towns are shrinking, so the important characteristics that were once unique to rural America are making their way into cities. However, when attempting to understand an entire society, one must examine all of its communities, including small towns and rural villages. Knowing the criteria used to create the original position would make affirming or refuting it a simpler task.

Issue Task 7

Claim: Governments must ensure that their major cities receive the financial support they need in order to thrive.

Reason: It is primarily in cities that a nation's cultural traditions are preserved and generated.

Write a response in which you discuss the extent to which you agree or disagree with the claim and the reason on which that claim is based.

Strategies

Combine the claim and reason into one statement using a subordinate clause.

In other words:

Because it is in cities that a nation's cultural traditions are preserved and generated, governments must ensure that their major cities receive the financial support they need in order to thrive.

What are the assumptions in the claim and reason? These will provide evidence that you can either affirm or refute in your argument.

a) Cities generate and preserve most of a nation's cultural traditions.

b) Small towns and rural areas do not generate or preserve a nation's cultural traditions.

c) Cities are unable to thrive without financial support from the government.

d) Cultural traditions should be preserved.

e) Funding cities in order to preserve cultural traditions is a valuable use of government money.

Next, create a statement that expresses an opposing point of view, using language similar to that in the original statement.

Opposing viewpoint:

Claim: Governments must ensure that communities of all sizes receive the financial support they need to thrive.

Reason: All communities help to generate and preserve a nation's cultural traditions.

What are the assumptions in the claim and reason? These will provide evidence that you can either affirm or refute in your argument.

a) No type of community should be ignored as a preserver of cultural traditions.

b) Cities and small towns should receive equal financial support as preservers of cultural traditions.

c) Some cultural traditions may disappear if certain types of communities are allowed to flounder financially.

Is there any other way to look at this issue? Can you qualify the original statement in some way? Is it possible to partially agree with the statement?

Alternative view:

Claim: Governments should not fund their major cities in order to preserve cultural traditions.

Reason: Cultural groups should be responsible for preserving their own traditions.

What are the assumptions in the alternative claim and reason?

a) Governments should not fund the preservation of cultural traditions.

b) Government should fund projects that benefit the greatest number of people rather than small groups of people.

c) Each cultural group should do what it takes to preserve its own traditions.

Sample Essay

America is a country of immigrants. Over the course of this country's brief history, groups or individuals have made their way to our shores to escape persecution, starvation, or any number of disasters. Language, religious, or other barriers led them to seek those from similar backgrounds, creating communities and neighborhoods where many cultural traditions have been preserved through several generations. These are traditions that they carried with them from their countries of origin. As a nation, America has very few original cultural traditions. The most notable of these is Thanksgiving. We also celebrate our own Independence Day on July fourth and Columbus Day in October. They were neither generated in major cities, nor are they preserved exclusively in major cities. Americans generate and preserve cultural traditions in communities both large and small. Whether these traditions help major cities to thrive is questionable, and whether government funding of their preservation is warranted is subject to debate.

I grew up in a part of Maine that had a significant number of people whose ancestors came from Sweden during the last half of the nineteenth century. In fact, my own ancestors made that journey and settled in Stockholm, obviously named for the capital of their homeland. These Swedes were principally farmers, and they cleared the heavily-forested land and grew crops amenable to a short growing season. They established Lutheran churches, married other Swedish immigrants and prepared meals in the Swedish culinary tradition. Eventually mills designed to manufacture products from the abundant timber were built along the stream that ran through town, and Acadian-French people moved to Stockholm to work in the mills. The schools, once populated by children whose surnames were Anderson, Johnson, and Soderberg now included Plourdes, Rossignols, and Doucettes. The inevitable occurred: French people fell in love with and married Swedish people. Today, there may not be more than a handful of residents who can claim unadulterated Swedish blood. Despite the decline in population and the diluting of the bloodlines, the Swedish community celebrates Midsommar every year. To mark the longest day of the year, residents and visitors alike dress in quaint Swedish costumes, decorate and raise a Maypole, perform Swedish folk dances and eat Swedish food. This is accomplished without the infusion of state or federal funds; volunteers from the community do it all. I'm sure it's all lovely. I wouldn't know because I've never attended the festivities. Even though half of my ancestors are of Swedish descent, I have never lived anywhere but America. I am an American, not a Swedish-American, nor, more correctly, a Swedish-Irish-English-Dutch-American. Because cultural traditions are unique to specific religions, races, or ethnicities, they tend to separate people rather than pull them together. These traditions help individual cultures, rather than entire communities, to thrive.

The vitality of America's major cities relies on factors other than the preservation of cultural traditions. Major cities or any community requires a sound infrastructure to ensure its survival. Without sufficient streets in good repair residents cannot go to work during the day or to places of entertainment in the evening. Without an efficient means of delivering water and eliminating waste, cities would become breeding grounds for disease. A lack of electricity would cripple all forms of industry. Major cities must provide access to health care and education to its residents. Any level of financial support on the part of the government should be allocated to projects that make living in major cities more comfortable. When residents are comfortable, they can pursue activities that help their communities to thrive.

Over recent decades, uniquely American cultural traditions have lost their significance. Thanksgiving has been reduced to a day to prepare for Black Friday, the kickoff to the Christmas shopping season. Stores open earlier than normal and offer desirable merchandise at drastically reduced prices. Entire families spend time on Thanksgiving plotting their shopping strategies. They camp out at stores or get up extra early to be first through the doors when they open, often pushing other bargain hunters out of the way. In 2012, some major chain stores actually opened in the evening on Thanksgiving Day. When America's citizens have so little regard for the country's traditions, the government would be unwise to provide funds to major cities in an attempt to preserve them.

Issue Task 8

Claim: When planning courses, educators should take into account the interests and suggestions of their students.

Reason: Students are more motivated to learn when they are interested in what they are studying.

Write a response in which you discuss the extent to which you agree or disagree with the claim and the reason on which that claim is based.

Strategies

Combine the claim and reason into one statement using a subordinate clause.

In other words:

Because students are more motivated to learn when they are interested in what they are studying, educators should take into account the interests and suggestions of their students when planning courses.

What are the assumptions present in the claim and reason? These will provide evidence that you can either affirm or refute.

a) Students are more motivated to learn material in which they are interested.

b) Students will be more successful when studying material in which they are interested.

c) Educators will be more effective when they teach material in which their students have some interest.

d) Students will be less successful when forced to study material in which they have little or no interest.

e) Educators will be less effective when teaching material in which their students have little or no interest.

f) Student motivation is extrinsic.

Next, create a statement that expresses the opposing view, using language similar to that in the original issue.

Opposing viewpoint:

Claim - When planning courses, educators should ignore the suggestions and interests of their students.

Reason - Students do not understand what they need to learn for success as adults.

What are the assumptions present in the claim and reason? These will provide evidence that you can either affirm or refute.

a) Educators have a better understanding of what students should study.

b) Student opinions and suggestions are not important.

c) Students lack the maturity to choose what they need to study.

Is there another way of looking at the claim and reason? Can both viewpoints be true or partially true?

Alternative viewpoint:

Claim - In some cases, educators should consider the suggestions and interests of their students when they plan their courses.

Reason - Students may have special needs or learning styles.

Examples:

Core Courses in college - students are required to take specified courses before selecting a major

Exploration - most students don't know what they want to study in college. Required courses in a variety of disciplines allow them to explore their options.

Sample Essay

When I was considering my choice of colleges to attend and the course of study to pursue, I was overwhelmed. Many of my classmates even said they were going to postpone going to college because they didn't know what they wanted to do, and it would be a waste of money to attend in that case. One of my teachers finally asked, "How will you discover what you want to do if you don't go to college?" I realized that I would have the opportunity to broaden my horizons by taking classes in subjects that, heretofore, I had not been exposed to. The world of higher education would become my oyster, and I was eager to partake. I was eighteen years old and hardly experienced enough to advise college professors about their courses. It was hardly my place to demand that college professors consider my interests or ask for my suggestions for planning their courses.

Like any aspect of life, an education should be balanced. A child, lacking knowledge and a sophisticated palate, would choose to eat hot dogs or macaroni and cheese every day. Such a diet, over a long period of time, would leave the child without vital nutrients to ensure his optimum physical health. Eventually he must add fruits and vegetables to his daily regimen. His mother must eventually override his interests and suggestions and consider his well being. Although the child may protest initially and leave his veggies on the plate, his hunger will eventually compel him to give them a try. As he grows, he may become involved with athletics. His desire to compete successfully may even lead him to research the best diet for his level of activity.

This same child will begin school around the age of five and decide that recess or coloring is his favorite daily activity. Should his teacher allow him to pursue his favorite activity all day every day, his first year of education will poorly prepare him for his second year. He may become proficient on the monkey bars and always color inside the lines, but he will not know his numbers or letters, leading to lack of success at the next grade level. In this case, his teacher must intervene, perhaps by making recess or coloring a reward for completing an academic activity. In the same way that veggies in his diet will improve his physical health, academic rigor in his classroom will improve his intellectual health. Working with numbers may lead him to discover a natural ability in math, or learning his first words may inspire him to become a voracious reader or prolific writer.

While most of us need parents or teachers to help us balance our physical and intellectual diets, some are capable of making those choices independent of older and wiser parents or counselors. One of my friends attended a private women's college with no core requirements. She could have taken four years of courses in just Italian, or just math, or just psychology if she so chose. In fact, she took courses in horseback riding and kayaking, which probably caused her parents to question their decision to let her attend this prestigious college. Eventually, my friend took a class, The Deaf Child, which met at a school for the deaf located just behind the campus. She uncovered an interest in speech and hearing science, and , after two years at the college, transferred to a large state university and earned an undergraduate degree in that field of study. She found her way by taking courses whose content had been proscribed by educators and developed a strong, healthy intellect.

It might be nice to have educators, employers and even parents take our interests and suggestions into account before making decisions that affect us. A number of problems arise from these considerations. In a classroom or workplace or family home, several disparate interests reside. Whose interests or suggestions are more worthy of consideration? Imagine the time lost by those in authority while attempting to accommodate everyone. Some students, employees, and children will be left as dissatisfied as if no one's interests had never been considered. A college course catalog provides opportunities for students to explore and develop new interests. Deciding on which courses to offer should be left up to the professors who must use their areas of expertise to develop the content of those courses.

Issue Task 9

Claim: We can usually learn much more from people whose views we share than from those whose views contradict our own.

Reason: Disagreement can cause stress and inhibit learning.

Write a response in which you discuss the extent to which you agree or disagree with the claim and the reason on which that claim is based.

Strategies

Combine the claim and reason into one statement using a subordinate clause.

In other words:

Because disagreement can cause stress and inhibit learning, we are more likely to learn from people whose views we share rather than those whose views contradict our own.

What are the assumptions in the claim and reason? These will provide evidence that you can either affirm or refute.

a) We can only learn from those with whom we agree.

b) We learn only when we are comfortable.

Opposing viewpoint:

Claim - We can usually learn more from people whose views contradict our own than from those with whom we agree.

Reason - Agreement causes complacency and inhibits learning.

What are the assumptions present in the claim and reason? These will provide evidence that you can either affirm or refute.

a) Other points of view offer new information.

b) Those with whom we agree echo what we already know or believe.

c) Without disagreement there is no learning.

Is there any other way to look at this issue? Can you qualify the original statement in some way? Is it possible to partially agree with the statement?

Alternative view:

Claim - We can learn from those whose views agree with our own as well as from those whose views contradict our own.

Reason - We don't have to agree with others to learn from them.

What are the assumptions present in the alternative claim and reason?

a) Every point of view has something to offer.

Examples:

Rumspringa - The year that Amish young people take off to live with the English. The Amish believe that exposure to the outside world makes those who return to the Amish life stronger members of the community.

High school debates - must know opposing viewpoint to strengthen support of one's own position

Politics - Decisions made by lawmakers do not always favor one party over another. Most laws result from considering both sides and reaching a compromise.

Sample Essay

If you do what you've always done, you'll get what you've always had. Limiting yourself to eating only what you've always eaten prevents you from sampling cuisines from all over the world and, perhaps, discovering your new favorite food. Selecting your next novel from the same genre that you've always read limits your exposure to the talents of thousands of writers. Exposing yourself to new foods, new authors, or new ideas can be stressful, but it will either change your life in some way or reaffirm the choices that you've already made.

The Amish, who live apart from modern society and spurn any conveniences, encourage their young people to participate in the tradition known as Rumspringa. Generally in their late teens, these young adults leave the comfort of their orderly communities and relocate to a city in order to live like the "English". At their own discretion, they make friends with those outside their faith, wear fashionable clothing, and attend parties where they may choose to drink alcoholic beverages. At the end of their year, they freely decide to return to the Amish lifestyle or remain in the secular world. The Amish elders understand that those who choose to return will become the strongest members of their society. Freely spurning modern technology to live a life of hard physical labor accomplished only with the help of work horses displays a firm dedication to the religion and lifestyle practiced by generations of their ancestors. Certainly there is some comfort in knowing what to expect of each day without the distractions of television, computers, and smart phones or the stress of maintaining the fast pace of life in the English world. They take pleasure in contributing to their community through the work of their hands and their faith in God rather than in updating their Facebook statuses or incessant text messages. They have likely learned many life lessons from those with whom they have fundamental disagreements.

An exit-level assessment at the high school I attended is a team debate carried out in front of the entire senior class. We were given a list of topics from which to choose and were then randomly assigned to teams. The greatest challenge came when we were told whether we would be arguing in the affirmative or the negative. Several members of each team were compelled to support a point of view with which they disagreed. Imagine the groans of protest! My group had to debate comprehensive versus abstinence-only sex education in public schools. I was selected to debate the position with which I disagreed. It was frustrating and stressful to develop a cogent argument to support this contrary point of view, but it did not prevent my learning about the strengths of that position. Although I did not change my opinion on the topic, I learned a lot about the other side of the debate and understood why it has merit. In fact, one is likely to learn more by tackling new and sometimes disagreeable information.

During the most recent presidential election, I watched my friends and family debate the suitability of the candidates by posting supposed facts on Facebook. I'm sure that they saw a posting by someone else, and they thought, "I agree. I'll repost this." Some of these postings, whether or not they aligned with my beliefs, seemed too pejorative to be true. On more than one occasion, I did some research and found, for example, that Michelle Obama does not have a greater number of personal assistants than former first ladies have had. Quotes ascribed to the president were taken out of context or said years before he became an elected official. Only by disagreeing with or, at the very least, questioning my Facebook friends did I come across information that was new to me.

Without change there is no progress. Without disagreement there is no change. Therefore, without disagreement, there is no progress. Had President Lincoln not disagreed with secessionists, America might still be a divided country. Had Galileo not disagreed with the Catholic Church, we might still think the Earth is the center of the Universe. Giants in the arts, literature, the humanities, and science have flouted the status quo, and we are better off as a result. This claim and reason are valid only for people who ignore history.

Issue Task 10

> *Young people should be encouraged to pursue long-term, realistic goals rather than seek immediate fame and recognition.*
>
> *Write a response in which you discuss the extent to which you agree or disagree with the recommendation and explain your reasoning for the position you take. In developing and supporting your position, describe specific circumstances in which adopting the recommendation would or would not be advantageous and explain how these examples shape your position.*

Strategies

Restate the issue perhaps by reversing the order of the sentence components.

In other words:

Rather than seek immediate fame and recognition, young people should be encouraged to pursue long-term realistic goals.

Determine what question is being answered by the statement. This will help you begin to think how you would answer it and whether or not you agree with the original statement.

Should young people pursue long-term goals or seek immediate fame and recognition?

Parts of the original statement that provide evidence that you can affirm or refute.

a) **young people** - They are less likely to have the necessary maturity or skills to create goals

b) **encouraged** - Provide reasons and information to help them rather than set the goals for them

c) **long-term** - Goals that will not be achieved quickly

d) **realistic** - Goals should be based on one's ability to achieve them

e) **immediate** - Right now or in the near future; in the context of the statement, it has a negative connotation

f) **fame** - Fame is a result of a variety of accomplishments, and, in this context, seems undesirable

g) **recognition** - Recognition implies acknowledgement of good deeds or accomplishments

Next, create a statement that expresses the opposing viewpoint, using language similar to that of the original statement.

Opposing viewpoint:

Young people should be encouraged to seek immediate fame and recognition rather than pursue long-term, realistic goals.

The evidence in this viewpoint is essentially the same as in the original. Is there any other way to look at this issue? Can you qualify the original statement in some way? Is it possible to partially agree with the statement?

Alternative viewpoint:

Young people should be encouraged to pursue long-term, realistic goals as well as immediate fame and recognition.

a) as well as - Both options should be available

List some circumstances under which each might be true.

Circumstances:

a) Advances in medicine occur as a result of long-range planning and study.

b) Business success derives from long-range planning.

c) A secure retirement requires planning and saving over many years.

d) Immediate fame is a suitable goal for professional athletes, whose careers are generally short-lived.

Sample Essay

For most young people, setting long-term, realistic goals is the route to lifetime success. Those who choose this route are less likely to experience failure and become discouraged. However, setting long-term, realistic goals is not the best choice for some, and notable exceptions exist today and throughout history that demonstrate the wisdom of their choices. Those with special talents may be better served by seeking immediate fame and recognition.

The world of professional sports is populated by stellar athletes who made the decision to seek immediate fame and recognition. It used to be that those seeking careers as professional athletes would first complete a college degree and, then, enter the draft. In recent years, it has become more common for those with high-level skills to leave college early or never attend at all and be drafted right out of high school. Kobe Bryant and LeBron James went directly from high school to the NBA. At the ripe old age of eighteen, each was making millions of dollars per year. Would four years of college hoops have made them better players? Perhaps not. They may have run the risk of career-ending injuries, ultimately ending any chance of signing multi-year, multi-million dollar contracts. Seeking immediate fame and recognition was the right decision for these two superstars, both of whom have won multiple NBA championships with their teams.

Examples abound in the world of the arts of those whose talents may not have been recognized or rewarded had they been advised to set realistic goals. Every year, hundreds of thousands of hopefuls audition for American Idol. Rather than testing their talents in small clubs or enduring rounds of auditions, these young singers take a single shot at the big time. Only one of them can win the prize, relegating the remainder to the ranks of also-rans. In the case of the winner and a select few of the top ten, great success ensues. In 2012, Phil Phillips won, and the song written for him to sing in the finale became the theme of the American gymnastics team at the London Olympics. Still a teenager, Phillips gained immediate fame and recognition. Had he not taken a chance on American Idol, he may have continued to sing in church and the school choir, and singing might have become a pleasant pastime in his adult life.

Situations do exist where long-term, realistic goals are more likely to insure success. Medical research comes to mind. As scientists search for cures or treatments for serious, even deadly, diseases or genetic conditions, they must meticulously test and retest, create scientific trials, and seek FDA approval before releasing new drugs on the market. This process can take many years, and virtually none of those individual scientists gains fame or recognition.

A young woman from my home town set a long-term goal for her life when she was a small child. She wanted to be an astronaut when she grew up. Toward that end, Jessica Meir worked hard in school and graduated as valedictorian of her class. She went on to Brown University and obtained her first degree. She completed research at the Scripps Oceanographic institute, becoming an aquanaut. Eventually, she attended the International Space University in Strasbourg, France. At the time of her selection as one of eight in the newest class of NASA astronauts she was an assistant professor of anesthesiology at Harvard. Now in her mid-thirties, Jessica has reached her lifelong goal by systematically setting a course that would lead her there. It is important to note that Jessica was not selected the first time she applied to become an astronaut, but she stayed the course and, eventually, reached her destination.

In reality, the vast majority of us benefit from setting long-term goals. The finish line is far in the future, and we will get there one step at a time. Making long-term, realistic goals will keep us from becoming discouraged or quitting altogether. Even very talented individuals sometimes spurn the chance for early fame and recognition in order to avoid the stress and public scrutiny that attend them. Young people should be encouraged to take the path that best suits their talents and circumstances.

Issue Task 11

Scientists and other researchers should focus their research on areas that are likely to benefit the greatest number of people.

Write a response in which you discuss the extent to which you agree or disagree with the recommendation and explain your reasoning for the position you take. In developing and supporting your position, describe specific circumstances in which adopting the recommendation would or would not be advantageous and explain how these examples shape your position.

Strategies

Restate the issue, perhaps by reversing the order of the sentence components.

In other words:

Areas that are likely to benefit the greatest number of people should be the focus of scientists and other researchers.

Determine what question is being answered by the statement. This will help you begin to think how you would answer it and whether or not you agree with the original statement.

On what areas should scientists and other researchers focus their research?

Parts of the original statement that provide evidence that you can affirm or refute.

a) **scientists** - This identifies someone with advanced education in some field of science.

b) **other researchers** - Does this mean researchers in fields other than science? Education, perhaps?

c) **focus** - Look closely at or select one subject

d) **likely** - This suggests probability rather than certainty

e) **benefit** - Scientists and other researchers should avoid areas that would cause harm. What type of benefit?

f) **the greatest number of people** - Areas of research that benefit a small number of people should be abandoned. They should also abandon research that might benefit animals.

Next, create a statement that expresses the opposing viewpoint, using language similar to that of the original statement.

Opposing viewpoint:

Scientists and other researchers should not focus only on areas that benefit the greatest number of people.

a) **not only** - Scientists and other researchers should work to benefit any size group.

Is there any other way to look at this issue? Can you qualify the original statement in some way? Is it possible to partially agree with the statement?

Alternative view:

Scientists and other researchers should first focus on areas that have the greatest urgency.

a) **first** - Scientists should prioritize the subjects of their research.

b) **greatest urgency** - Scientists must decide what can be postponed and what must be addressed immediately.

Examples:

Global warming or climate change - This qualifies as both urgent and having an effect on the greatest number of people.

AIDS - Failure to stop the spread or a cure threatens large numbers of people.

Autism Spectrum Disorders - The dramatic increase in the number of children diagnosed affects both families and schools.

Polio - Although it did not affect large numbers of people, scientists were compelled to eradicate it.

Sample Essay

It is generally true that people make important choices in their lives based on deep interest or abiding passion. They may be influenced by a personal connection. A scientist, for example, may have watched his mother die from breast cancer, and, as a result, he dedicates his working life to discovering a cure. Another may have a sibling diagnosed with type I diabetes at an early age and focuses his research on putting an end to that life-long, debilitating condition. A third may have had a beloved neighbor with Down syndrome and dedicates his career to discover a means to repair or prevent chromosomal disorders. On the other hand, when scientists and researchers are required to work only on problems that affect the greatest number of people, they may be less likely to proceed with the required fervor to effect timely and far-reaching results. Scientists and other researchers should focus on areas that enable them to work tirelessly to relieve the ills of humanity, regardless of the number of people who benefit from their endeavors.

Scientists do not have crystal balls. They cannot predict which subject of research may ultimately benefit a great number of people. At one time, autism spectrum disorders were thought to be relatively rare, and little was done to improve the lives of those affected. They were isolated and given a pessimistic prognosis for any improvement in their condition or quality of life. Over the past few years, the rise in the number of those diagnosed with ASD has experienced a meteoric rise. Doctors claim that one in eighty children will be diagnosed with some form of autism, placing enormous burdens on families and schools. No one in the 1970's could have predicted that cases of ASD would increase at such a rapid rate. Once excluded from the world of work and education, most that have some form of autism today complete college and become productive citizens. Had scientists and other researchers ignored autism because it affected a supposedly low number of individuals, the progress that has been made would have been delayed by several decades, and our society would be poorer without the contributions of these people.

In the 1980's a disease emerged that created great concern and controversy around the world. When AIDS first came to the public's attention, it was regarded as a "gay" disease, present almost exclusively in homosexual men who had multiple sexual partners. The poster boy for this plague was Rock Hudson, the once strapping, handsome leading man on both the big and small screens of America. The world watched as images of his haggard and wasted physique appeared in magazines and read of his desperate trips to France to seek any kind of treatment for his illness. His death provided fodder for those who think of homosexuality as an abomination; this plague was God's retribution. These attitudes and the apparently narrow scope of the disease may have delayed research for an effective treatment. When cases of AIDS began showing up in other segments of the population and its spread became rapid, researchers began to accelerate the process of finding a treatment or cure. Had the medical community relegated AIDS research to the back burner because it appeared to affect only people who engaged in risky behavior, the advances in treatment that prolong life and, in some cases, cure the disease might still exist only in the future.

Of great concern to scientists today is climate change. Most believe that human interaction with the environment has created a variety of issues, including the hole in the ozone and the melting of the polar icecaps. Former Vice President, Al Gore, has been an outspoken critic of human practices that have led to global warming and has gone around the world with his documentary, An Inconvenient Truth, advocating for change. No other issue has effects as far reaching as this; every living human, animal, and plant is threatened in some way. Droughts, floods, desertification, and extinction challenge every society around the globe. No other issue affects a greater number of people, and failure to correct or reverse these changes spells doom for coastal communities as well as plant and animal species. Failure to focus research on the environment will have a deleterious effect on great numbers of people around the world.

It is easy to identify concerns that currently affect the largest number of people. Focusing on those issues may cause scientists and other researchers to overlook problems that, although small now, may eventually have a negative impact on considerable populations. The world is smaller today. The ability of people to travel quickly and frequently to all corners of the globe makes once isolated issues a concern for everyone on the planet. Scientists and other researchers should be encouraged to perform their work in ways that benefit any group of humans.

Issue Task 12

The human mind will always be superior to machines because machines are only tools of human minds.

Write a response in which you discuss the extent to which you agree or disagree with the statement and explain your reasoning for the position you take. In developing and supporting your position, you should consider ways in which the statement might or might not hold true and explain how these considerations shape your position.

Strategies

Restate the issue, perhaps by reversing the order of the sentence components.

In other words

Because machines are only tools of human minds, the human mind will always be superior to machines.

Determine what question is being answered by the statement. This will help you begin to think how you would answer it and whether or not you agree with the original statement.

Why is the human mind superior to machines?

Parts of the original statement that provide evidence that you can affirm or refute.

a) **always** - This absolute leaves no room for other options. Is it possible for something to be always true? Never true?

b) **superior** - A superior position is above any other. It is higher, better.

c) **only** - This can imply exclusivity, e.g.., the only one. It also suggests a lack, e.g., only enough for two.

d) **tools** - Humans have developed tools to make tasks easier. The ability to use tools has elevated some species and ensures their survival.

e) **machines** - They are inanimate objects designed to serve man.

Next, create a statement that expresses the opposing viewpoint, using language similar to that of the original statement.

Opposing viewpoint:

Even though man has created machines, his mind is not always superior to machines.

Parts of the statement that provide evidence that you can affirm or refute.

a) **even though** – This suggests exemptions or conditions under which the original statement may not be true.

b) **not always** – This is also a conditional phrase.

Alternative viewpoint:

Man's failure to develop his mind can lead to the superiority of machines over man.

a) **failure to develop** – not learning how to use or manipulate sophisticated machines

Examples:

2001: A Space Odyssey – Hal begins to make independent decisions.

Watson, created by IBM to play Jeopardy!

Many people never learned to program their VCR's.

Sample Essay

When humans learned how to use tools, they increased their chances of survival. Humans were able to hunt more efficiently and plant crops, ensuring a food supply. Pulleys, levers, and wheels enabled men to lift heavy objects, move objects, and build shelters. Simple machines and tools were the servants of man. Over time, man modified his early tools and machines, and, by the middle of the twentieth century, humans were using tools and machines to accomplish virtually every daily task. Man had made all of these machines and was, therefore, superior to them. They did only what humans made them to do. For the most part, they still do, but the advent of Artificial Intelligence may change that.

In 1968, 2001 A Space Odyssey introduced audiences to Hal, a computer that had some human characteristics. Initially, a tool used by space travelers Dave and Frank, Hal begins to behave independently of them. Frank and Dave eventually become concerned enough to hatch a plot that will deactivate Hal. Hal foils the plot and reveals to Dave that the precautions he and Frank took to discuss their plan out of Hal's hearing were futile, as Hal can read lips. Forty years ago, no one had a computer at home, so Hal's independent actions may have seemed both fantastic and frightening to movie audiences.

Two years ago, Jeopardy! fans tuned in to watch Watson, a computer designed with artificial intelligence, compete against two of the show's top winners. Despite some hiccups, Watson beat the former champs, including Ken Jennings, who won more than seventy games in his reign as champion. Although Watson, named for the original founder of IBM, had been designed and programmed by humans, he was able to think independently when answering each question on the show. He was not connected to the Internet, and, therefore, could not search for correct answers. Watson functioned like a thinking human brain.

Even though most of us have not had encounters with Artificial Intelligence, we have purchased machines that demonstrate our limits. When VCR's became readily available, nearly everyone applauded the ability to watch popular movies in the comfort of our own homes. Programming the machine, however, was beyond the skill of many homeowners. As a result, most VCR's sat on the shelf flashing 12:00 for the lifetime of the device.

Throughout the history of man, machines, both simple and complex, have been the tools of man. In fact, our sophisticated use of tools is what sets us apart from other animal species. It is difficult for those living in the twenty-first century to imagine what life was like for humans without the machines that we use today. We can only imagine the time and labor involved in planting and harvesting crops before the advent of the cotton gin and the McCormack reaper, let alone the diesel-powered farm vehicles we see today. The working woman would not exist were it not for the labor-saving devices in her home: washing machines and dryers, vacuum cleaners and dishwashers. Today's students would find it quaint to complete math assignments without advanced calculators and English compositions without computers. Many schools have even gone paperless as students can submit their work online. For the purpose of making daily tasks easier, machines remain inferior to humans.

While it is true that the advanced machines that make our lives easier would not exist without the minds of men who created them, our mindless use of them may be our downfall. Little thought goes into accomplishing either simple or complex tasks. Humans today run on autopilot. Without much consideration, we load the dishwasher, start the clothes washer, and set the house alarm before heading out the door to get into our cars that apply the brakes automatically if something is behind us as we back out of the driveway and parallel park themselves when we reach our destinations. In many respects, every machine we own in turn owns us. We must clean them, maintain them, fuel them, and insure them. We have created a symbiotic rather than dominant relationship with the machines in our lives today. How our relationship with machines evolves will determine whether or not the human mind will remain superior to them.

Issue Task 13

Governments should not fund any scientific research whose consequences are unclear.

Write a response in which you discuss your views on the policy and explain your reasoning for the position you take. In developing and supporting your position, you should consider the possible consequences of implementing the policy and explain how these consequences shape your position.

NOTE: The above topic has wording similar to Issue Task 3 of GRE Analytical Writing Solutions to the Real Essay Topics - Book 1. However, if you read carefully you will notice that the task instructions are different. Hence, it is very important to read the topic as well as its instructions completely before you start to write your response.

Strategies

Restate the issue, perhaps by reversing the order of the sentence components.

In other words:

When the consequences of scientific research are unclear, governments should not fund it.

Determine what question is being answered by the statement. This will help you begin to think how you would answer it and whether or not you agree with the original statement.

Should governments fund scientific research whose consequences are unclear?

Parts of the original statement that provide evidence that you can affirm or refute.

a) **Governments** - This likely refers to national governments, although state governments and local governments may contribute financially to some research.

b) **scientific research** - This implies any field of science: medicine, chemistry, physics, etc.

c) **consequences** - They can be negative or positive.

d) **unclear** – Inconclusive

Next, create a statement that expresses the opposing viewpoint, using language similar to that of the original statement.

Opposing viewpoint:

Governments should fund scientific research even when the consequences are unclear.

a) **even when** - Even implies fairness or equality, no exceptions

Is there any other way to look at this issue? Can you qualify the original statement in some way? Is it possible to partially agree with the statement?

Alternative viewpoint:

Governments should fund scientific research whose consequences are unclear when the subject of the research benefits a

significant portion of the population.

a) **benefits a significant portion of the population** – Small, specific research projects having unclear consequences should not be funded

Examples:

a) Space exploration has created benefits for humans in several areas.

b) The Manhattan Project ultimately ended WWII.

c) Consequences of implementing the policy

d) Saving money to use for other purposes

e) Discouraging research of any kind

f) Loss of life

Sample Essay

Life is full of uncertainty. If humans demanded guarantees, they would not get up in the morning and leave their homes for work, school, or shopping. There is no guarantee that a businessman's car will not be hit by a speeding truck as he backs out of his driveway. There is no guarantee that a child will not be abducted on the way home from school. There is no guarantee that a wife will not have her purse stolen from her shopping cart in the grocery store. If we considered all of the uncertainties inherent in our routines, we would be immobilized. If the government agreed to fund only research with clear consequences, research would stagnate and the progress of the human condition along with it.

During WWII, the United States government funded research into the potential development of a powerful new type of weapon. The Manhattan Project was created with no guarantees that a nuclear bomb could or would be developed in time to make a difference in the outcome of the war. Housed in a variety of secret locations across the country, scientists worked separately on disparate tasks that included isolating plutonium and creating a delivery system for the weapon. Everyone knows that the war with Japan effectively ended when atomic bombs were dropped on the cities of Hiroshima and Nagasaki in August of 1945. The US believes that the destruction in Japan saved the lives of more than 100,000 Americans. Initially intended to cause destruction and loss of life, the results of the work done on the Manhattan Project have created important applications for peacetime. Nuclear medicine focuses on both diagnosis and treatment of disease in order to save lives. Neither the malevolent nor the benevolent aspects of nuclear research could have been guaranteed, but the government funded it anyway.

In the early 1960's, in reaction to the Soviet's launching of Sputnik, President Kennedy promised that, by the end of the decade, the United States would put a man on the moon. The space race was on. The Russians put the first man into space; the Americans created the first manned vehicle to orbit the earth. The moon still seemed far away. Today, there is not an American alive who does not know the name and achievement of Neil Armstrong, the first man to set foot on the moon. That happened in 1969. Forty four years later, there is no colony or industry on the moon. It would appear that, on the surface, the government wasted its money on a venture whose consequences were unclear. However, the tangential benefits of the space race are numerous and have changed all of our lives. The hundreds of thousands of humans who fly every day benefit from increased aviation safety, a direct result of sending vehicles beyond the Earth's atmosphere. Because the government funded NASA, none of its discoveries or products could be proprietary. They must share them. Dr. Michael DeBakey teamed with a NASA engineer to develop the first artificial heart pump that could be used to keep a patient alive until a suitable heart for transplant became available. The government generously funded an agency whose research outcomes were uncertain but whose accomplishments went far beyond initial expectations.

Today's world is afflicted by problems too critical to postpone action on. In fact, further delay could be fatal. Although many people may be weary of the dire warnings associated with global warming or even doubt the veracity of such claims, much evidence exists that changes in the Earth's temperatures have had devastating effects on people's health, the ability to grow sufficient food supplies, and sustaining some wildlife habitats. The hole in the ozone layer has caused an alarming increase in skin cancers. Spreading desertification has consumed land previously used to grow food. The polar bear faces extinction as ice caps melt. It is clear to oncologists, agronomists, and nature conservancy groups that research must continue or commence to solve these problems. To ensure the survival of all of Earth's inhabitants, governments around the globe must provide at least a portion of the funding for researching solutions to these problems.

The outcome of research is not clear until the process has been completed. The nature of research entails creating a hypothesis and determining its validity. Some succeed; some fail. The benefits of the successes outweigh the expense of those that fail. Adopting the original policy would lead to no funding of scientific research.

Issue Task 14

Knowing about the past cannot help people to make important decisions today.

Write a response in which you discuss the extent to which you agree or disagree with the statement and explain your reasoning for the position you take. In developing and supporting your position, you should consider ways in which the statement might or might not hold true and explain how these considerations shape your position.

NOTE: The above topic has wording similar to Issue Task 29 of GRE Analytical Writing Solutions to the Real Essay Topics Book 1. However, if you read carefully you will notice that the task instructions are different. Hence, it is very important to read the topic as well as its instructions completely before you start to write your response.

Strategies

Restate the issue, perhaps by reversing the order of the sentence components.

In other words:

Making important decisions today is not affected by knowledge about the past.

Determine what question is being answered by the statement. This will help you begin to think how you would answer it and whether or not you agree with the original statement.

Does knowing about the past help people to make important decisions today?

Parts of the original statement that provide evidence that you can affirm or refute.

a) **Knowing** – does not imply understanding

b) **past** – any time previous

c) **cannot help** – inability

d) **important** – some significance is attached

e) **decisions** – Usually arrived at after considering facts and alternatives

Next, create a statement that expresses the opposing viewpoint, using language similar to that of the original statement.

Opposing viewpoint:

Knowing about the past can help people make important decisions today.

a) **can** – expresses the opposite ability of the original position

Is there any other way to look at this issue? Can you qualify the original statement in some way? Is it possible to partially agree with the statement?

Alternative viewpoint:

Knowing about the past does not always help people make better decisions in the present.

a) **not always** – Using the past to make decisions does not always lead to good decisions.

b) **better** – People do make the same mistakes even when they know the poor results that occurred in the past.

Examples:

a) The Great Gatsby

b) Hangovers

c) Touching a hot stove

Sample Essay

We have all been warned by the oft-repeated aphorism, those who cannot remember the past are condemned to repeat it. Past experiences on both a national and personal level should serve as lessons that inform decisions and choices in the present. At the very least, the past can serve as a point of reference. The conflict arises when people don't understand the past.

F. Scott Fitzgerald wrote what many claim to be the greatest American novel ever written, The Great Gatsby. The eponymous main character spent his early years attempting to escape his past. Ashamed of his working-class roots, James Gatz changed his name and created semi-fictional curriculum vitae. While Gatsby served in WWI, the love of his life, Daisy Fay, married Tom Buchanan and proceeded to live in the lap of luxury in an upper class community on Long Island. After the war, Gatsby amassed a fortune in some unspecified, illegal business venture and used his ill-gotten gains in an attempt to win Daisy back. When his neighbor, Nick Caraway, became complicit in Gatsby's scheme, he admonished Gatsby that one cannot repeat the past. Gatsby replies, "Not repeat the past? Of course you can." The sad fact is that Gatsby not only believed it but also was able to imagine that the intervening years never existed. As a result, Jay Gatsby was unable to use the knowledge of his past with Daisy to make considered decisions in the present. His gleaming mansion, his hand-tailored shirts, his extravagant parties, and his quest for Daisy ended in a preventable tragedy.

My mother's favorite movie of all time is Dr. Zhivago, a tale of forbidden love set in Russia during the Communist revolution. The audience is transported as the Zhivago's lose the privileges they enjoyed in czarist Russia and are reduced to living in a small apartment inhabited by the great unwashed of society. They watch the handsome, charismatic Yuri fall in love with the beautiful Lara and their escape to the frosty country home where the young doctor feverishly writes poetry. For her own sake and safety, Yuri relinquishes Lara and makes his way on foot across the frozen tundra, compromising his own health along the way. The movie ends as Dr. Zhivago suffers a fatal heart attack while trying to exit a bus after seeing Lara on the street. Despite having seen it many times, my mother never misses a chance to see it again when it airs on television. If you were to ask her why she has seen it so many times, she will tell you that "this time", it will end differently. Dr. Zhivago and Lara will reunite.

Both Jay Gatsby and my mother exemplify our inability to use the past to inform our decisions in the present. Man's weakness is his inability or unwillingness to intellectualize events that occurred in the past. We are either hopelessly optimistic or stubbornly arrogant. Humans believe that the same disaster couldn't possibly occur again or that they will, by sheer dint of force, make events turn out differently despite approaching a problem in the same way. The Mississippi River, for example, floods on a regular basis, and many homes in its path are destroyed. The residents who have watched their homes and belongings float away vow to rebuild in the same place. This stubborn resolve, seen by some as courageous, is foolhardy and puts lives as well as property at risk.

Experience should be the best teacher, and in some cases, it is. The child who burns his hand on a hot stove will likely not touch it a second time. The tot who is bitten by a strange dog will shy away from the next one. On the other hand, a college student who suffers a hangover after a night of partying will not eschew the behavior that caused it when a party rolls around the next weekend. People choose what they want to remember. Humans are prone to remember what they want to and disregard the warnings that interfere with their own desires.

Issue Task 15

Claim: The best test of an argument is its ability to convince someone with an opposing viewpoint.

Reason: Only by being forced to defend an idea against the doubts and contrasting views of others does one really discover the value of that idea.

Write a response in which you discuss the extent to which you agree or disagree with the claim and the reason on which that claim is based.

Strategies

Combine the claim and reason into one statement using a subordinate clause.

In other words:

Because one cannot discover the value of an idea without defending it, the best test of an argument is its ability to convince someone with an opposing viewpoint.

What are the assumptions stated or implied in the claim and reason? These will provide evidence that you can refute or affirm in your argument.

a) Changing someone's mind is proof that you are right.

b) Ideas have no value unless you are forced to defend them.

c) One's ideas have no intrinsic value.

d) The value of one's ideas is created by others.

Opposing viewpoint:

Claim - The ability to convince someone with an opposing viewpoint is not the best test of an argument.

Reason – The argument may not be based on the best information.

Is there any other way to look at this issue? Can you qualify the original statement in some way? Is it possible to partially agree with the statement?

Alternative viewpoint:

Claim -One test of an argument is its ability to convince someone with an opposing viewpoint.

Reason- Defending an idea against the doubts and contrasting views of others is not more valid than other tests.

Examples:

a) Debates

b) My own state governor

Sample Essay

It is satisfying and self affirming to be able to make someone accept our point of view. Nothing feels as good as being right and having others admit it. Problems can arise when trying to convince another that one's point of view is the correct one. The proponents of an argument may use facts selectively or manipulate conditions in order to strengthen the position. Those having an opposing point of view may concede simply to put an end to the harangue of the other party. If one believes deeply in an idea, he or she should welcome the opportunity to examine the argument more closely.

I can appreciate an argument even when it fails to change my mind if I observe that its creator has researched his position and has used logic and verifiable facts and statistics to support it. When I was in high school, I participated in the debating club. The purpose of each debate was not to change anyone else's opinion but to create and deliver the most compelling argument. Topics, positions, and team roles were assigned in a random manner, and I found myself on more than one occasion having to defend a point of view with which I did not agree. This did not prevent my winning more debates than I lost. I spent hours researching, compiling statistics and evidence that my opponents would find difficult to refute. While doing so, I came to appreciate others' views on controversial topics and understand why they would defend them.

The governor of my state appears to believe that right is might. He has spent the two-and-a-half years of his tenure arguing that the state should allow more charter schools. His contention is that public education in the state is failing to meet the needs of its students, and the students should have more choice in selecting a high school. In order to prove the correctness of his argument, he has taken several steps to undermine public education. On one hand, he proposed deep cuts in financing of public education, while, on the other hand, he advocated public funding of private and religious schools. Many of his opponents claim that he has used flawed evidence to promote his contention that private and religious schools provide better educations. In fact, those schools do not have to meet the same standards or administer the same tests as the public schools must. Most recently, the Department of Education assigned letter grades from A-F to each public school in the state. Less than a month before releasing the grades, the Commissioner of Education revealed the criteria on which the grades would be based, giving schools no time to address those criteria. A significant portion of the grade derived from standardized test scores in math and English from the previous year's administration of those tests. In addition, the grades were assigned on a bell curve, meaning that a specific number of schools would receive A's, and roughly the same number would receive F's. When the grades revealed that only nine schools in the state had received a grade of A, the governor was able to say that he had been right all along about the poor quality of public education in the state. The governor's actions illuminate a weakness in attempting to defend an argument. One may be tempted to manipulate conditions in order to prove its veracity.

The best test of an argument may be the ability to both understand and appreciate the other point of view while remaining steadfastly convinced of one's own position. In matters of faith, for example, leaders of any religious denomination believe that the faithful should question the tenets of their belief system. Only by searching for answers can one become stronger in his or her beliefs.

Issue Task 16

> *Some people believe that in order to thrive, a society must put its own overall success before the well-being of its individual citizens. Others believe that the well-being of a society can only be measured by the general welfare of all its people.*
>
> *Write a response in which you discuss which view more closely aligns with your own position and explain your reasoning for the position you take. In developing and supporting your position, you should address both of the views presented.*

Strategies

This issue already has two points of view. Begin by treating them separately. Restate the first opinion by reversing the order of the sentence components.

In other words:

A society must put its own overall success before the well-being of its individual citizens in order to thrive.

Determine what question is being answered by the statement. This will help you begin to think how you would answer it and whether or not you agree with the original statement.

Should a society put its overall success before the well-being of its individual citizens in order to thrive?

Parts of the original statement that provide evidence that you can affirm or refute.

a) **some people** - This qualifier lets the reader know that the opinion is not universal. There is another side.

b) **thrive** - This is a stronger idea than merely existing. Thriving involves great success.

c) **society** - What comprises a society? A society is a group with common characteristics or goals. It can be large or small.

d) **before** - Put overall success of a society chronologically ahead of individual needs.

e) **well-being** - What type of well-being? Physical? Fiscal? Emotional?

f) **individual citizens** - Each member of society separately

Opposing viewpoint:

Others believe that the well-being of a society can only be measured by the general welfare of all its people.

Restate the second opinion by reversing the order of the sentence components.

In other words:

The general welfare of all its people is the measure of a society's well-being.

Parts of the statement that provide evidence that you can affirm or refute.

a) **general welfare** - What does this include? Does it refer to basic needs like food, shelter? What about employment, health care, safety?

b) **measure** – In this case, determining factor

Is there any other way to look at this issue? Can you qualify the original statement in some way? Is it possible to partially agree with the statement?

Alternative viewpoint:

The well-being of a society can be measured by the general welfare of most of its people.

a) **most** – some people's needs will not be met

Examples:

The working poor

Mother Theresa

How ignoring the poorest, least capable in a society affects progress

Sample Essay

A nation's general welfare depends on the welfare of its individual citizens. When every citizen can free himself from dependency on government assistance and make his own contributions to the economy, the entire population can benefit. The tax contributions of others can be abated leaving them with more discretionary income to purchase goods and services, funds to educate their children, and provide preventive health care for all family members. The providers of goods and services will react to increases in business by hiring more workers and ordering more inventory or raw materials. The trend is obvious; the general well-being of a society improves when all of its members are given the opportunity to advance.

Immigrants to the United States still believe its streets are paved in gold and that opportunities abound for anyone who is willing to work hard. However, many Americans fall into the demographic known as the working poor. According to research from earlier this year, America's total personal wealth is about $54 trillion. One percent of the population controls forty percent of that total. Eighty percent of the population controls a puny seven percent of the wealth. A significant portion of US citizens live below the poverty line which is set at an income ranging from $11,000-$12,000 per year for a single person, less than someone working full time for the federal minimum wage of $7.25/hour. Those living at or near the poverty line must apply for Medicaid in their states of residence, a program supported by tax dollars. Those same individuals likely need food stamps, and they probably qualify for federally supplemented rental properties.

In her book, Nickel and Dimed, Barbara Ehrenreich writes about the working poor in America after experiencing first-hand the lives they lead. She left the comfort of her home in Florida to take on menial jobs in three locations around the country. She rented places to live based on the wages she would earn at each job with a goal of saving enough money to pay the next month's rent. In most cases, she had to work a second job just to make ends meet. She came to admire the hardworking people – mostly women- that she worked with and recorded their stories along with her own in her book. She came to the conclusion that the workers who do the jobs that make life easier for everyone else were undervalued. These people didn't have paid sick days or health insurance, so they went to work even when they were sick or injured. Losing a day's pay spelled financial disaster for them. When citizens of a society cannot afford adequate health care or earn wages that do not allow them to scrape out more than a meager living, they cannot contribute to the overall success of a society.

Today, the citizens of our country are engaged in a great debate about health care. President Obama has led the crusade for providing affordable health insurance for everyone in the United States. His opponents believe that the Affordable Health Care Act will be too costly, that businesses will suffer from being compelled to offer coverage to their employees, and that jobs will be lost. Republicans, for the most part, want to de-fund Obamacare, and to that end, Senator Cruz delivered the fourth-longest filibuster in the history of the country in an effort to convince his fellow senators to vote against funding the program. The deadlock in Washington threatens to shut down government. On the surface, it appears that the Republicans believe that the overall success of society does not depend on the well-being of its individual citizens, while the Democrats and the President believe that the well-being of every individual in the country will ensure overall success for America.

When a country must supplement the basic lifestyles of a significant number of its citizens, that country cannot be considered to be thriving. When the general welfare of its citizens depends on raising taxes on middle and high income earners and postponing improvements to its infrastructure or military or educational institutions, the country begins to lose the ability to transport people and goods efficiently, to protect its citizens from enemies both foreign and domestic, and to provide skilled workers for essential occupations. Those whose general welfare is below par are a drain on society, and only by elevating them can the country achieve overall success.

Issue Task 17

Claim: Any piece of information referred to as a fact should be mistrusted, since it may well be proven false in the future.

Reason: Much of the information that people assume is factual actually turns out to be inaccurate.

Write a response in which you discuss the extent to which you agree or disagree with the claim and the reason on which that claim is based.

Strategies

Combine the claim and the reason into one statement using a subordinate clause.

In other words:

Because much of the information that people assume is factual actually turns out to be inaccurate, any piece of information referred to as a fact should be mistrusted since it may well be proven false in the future.

What are the assumptions stated or implied in the claim and reason? These will provide evidence that you can refute or affirm in your argument.

a) Most facts will eventually be proven false.

b) One shouldn't trust what others claim to be true.

c) People are generally willing to believe what others say is true.

Opposing viewpoint:

Claim – No piece of information referred to as fact should be mistrusted, because it will hold true in the future.

Reason – Much of the information that people assume is factual actually is.

Alternative viewpoint:

Claim – Not every piece of information referred to as fact should be mistrusted, since some may well be proven false in the future.

Reason – A considerable amount of the information that people assume is factual actually is.

Examples:

Gossip

Campaign Rhetoric

Advances in science

Sample Essay

A healthy dose of skepticism is recommended when digesting a meal of facts delivered by someone else. In most cases, however, one should trust that those who have expertise in a specific field have done due diligence before making claims they presume to be true. Over time and with improved technology, new discoveries may appear that alter or contradict the current facts, but that doesn't mean they weren't true for the time and conditions under which they were espoused.

Some facts are true in the context in which they appear, but the reporters of such facts have cherry-picked them to serve their own purposes. This is never more obvious than during a presidential election. Social media makes these "facts" spread like wildfire, and the uninformed willingly accept them as gospel, especially if they coincide with their own political leanings. One of the most pervasive claims during the last presidential election was based on a chart depicting the yearly salaries of the President and members of Congress. The chart intended to inflame readers by stating that those individuals get that salary for life. While the dollar amounts were correct, the duration of said salaries was not. The President, senators and representatives get a pension based on their salaries. Another fact intended to shame Michelle Obama for having 26 assistants. What a waste of taxpayer money! A little research reveals that Laura Bush and other First Ladies had similar numbers of assistants. Displaying a little mistrust concerning facts presented for political purposes is wise.

Gossip is, perhaps, the most egregious misuse of facts. Generally repeated sotto voce, gossip can easily be misheard or misinterpreted. The listener then hurries off to spread the facts as he or she understood them. By the time the inflammatory remarks return to the subject of them, there is little truth remaining. In the case of gossip, the issue's original claim and reason hold true, not just for the sake of accuracy but for the protection of those subjected to vicious gossip. Rumors have characteristics in common with gossip. However, while gossip is never intended to spread good news, rumors may be used to disseminate both good and bad information, and their effect can be just as harmful as gossip. I live in a small city that was devastated when a nearby Air Force base closed. It had been rumored that the base would close several times over the years. Each time that the rumors began, local citizens would become despondent with worry over their futures. A Save Loring Committee worked tirelessly to keep the base from closing and succeeded twice. When the rumors began the third time, the locals refused to believe them, and believed the more positive rumors that, once again, the base would remain open. It was like the little boy who cried wolf. As in the fable, the wolf, in the form of BRAC, did finally make an appearance, and the citizens of my town were caught unawares.

Some facts that have been disproved have little or no effect, either positive or negative, on the course of human development. In recent history, Pluto has lost its status as a planet. It was always a little suspect, anyway. So our solar system is reduced to eight planets. This fact reversal has no effect on the way the world proceeds or stands as an argument that one should mistrust factual information. A much earlier astronomical reversal, however, did have an impact on the world. The Catholic Church believed the Earth to be the center of the universe. Since God had created the Earth and all of the creatures in it, it must be the most important of His creations. Hence, the sun and other planets must be inferior and show obeisance to the Earth by revolving around it. In the sixteenth century, Copernicus developed a model that disproved the geocentric theory and validated the heliocentric theory that had been proposed centuries before. Even though the Church was wrong about the solar system, one should not necessarily mistrust everything that the Church proclaims to be fact.

Every day begins with the immutable fact that the sun will rise in the East and ends when the sun sets in the West. Much of what happens in that span of time is open to interpretation, but the average human will not question the events that occur or the facts they hear. Those who do so relinquish the ability to simply enjoy the day that they have been given. The habit of mistrusting those in authority leads to a life filled with uncertainty.

Issue Task 18

Claim: Nations should suspend government funding for the arts when significant numbers of their citizens are hungry or unemployed.

Reason: It is inappropriate - and, perhaps, even cruel - to use public resources to fund the arts when people's basic needs are not being met.

Write a response in which you discuss the extent to which you agree or disagree with the claim and the reason on which that claim is based.

Strategies

Combine the claim and the reason into one statement using a subordinate clause.

In other words:

Because it is inappropriate to use public resources to fund the arts when people's basic needs are not being met, nations should suspend government funding for the arts when significant numbers of their citizens are hungry or unemployed.

What are the assumptions stated or implied in the claim and reason? These will provide evidence that you can refute or affirm in your argument.

a) Supporting the arts is less important than feeding the hungry or creating jobs.

b) The arts are not a basic need.

c) The amount of money dedicated to funding the arts is equal to the amount needed to feed the hungry and create jobs.

d) Eliminating funding for the arts will alleviate hunger and unemployment.

e) Funding for the arts can be resumed when people's basic needs are being met.

Opposing viewpoint:

Claim: Nations should provide funding for the arts even when significant numbers of their citizens at hungry or unemployed.

Reason: It is appropriate - and perhaps necessary - to fund the arts even when people's basic needs are not being met.

What are the assumptions stated or implied in the claim and reason? These will provide evidence that you can refute or affirm in your argument.

a) A nation's artistic accomplishments are as important as the welfare of its citizens.

Alternative viewpoint:

Claim: Nations should reduce government funding for the arts when significant numbers of their citizens are hungry or unemployed.

Reason: Reducing the funding may help alleviate hunger and unemployment until they reach acceptable levels.

What are the assumptions stated or implied in the claim and reason? These will provide evidence that you can refute or affirm in your argument.

a) A temporary reduction in funding is the best course.

b) Eliminating funding for the arts altogether is unnecessary.

Sample Essay

Some may believe that art is a luxury and has little to do with people's basic needs. When a country is facing economic challenges, it seems easy and logical to eliminate or reduce funding for the arts. Even on a local level, school boards often recommend cutting art classes and music programs when budgets are strained. Others contend that the arts are an essential part of life and education. Evidence exists in both history and science that supports sustaining the arts even when funding them seems inappropriate.

During the Great Depression, President Roosevelt and Congress created numerous projects that put unemployed Americans to work. Among them was the Federal Writers Project which paid both professional and amateur writers to produce pieces that reflected the culture of the country. Despite criticism, the project continued for four years, eventually employing teachers, librarians, and college graduates. The result was a collection of oral histories, state informational guides, children's books, ethnographies, and other works. National funding for the arts during America's greatest financial crisis actually alleviated unemployment and preserved our cultural identity.

It is difficult to imagine what other countries would know about America or what Americans would know or understand about other countries without the arts. Before the advent of photography, painters provided depictions of the great cities of Europe as well as scenes of daily life. Writers like Charles Dickens illuminated the turmoil in Paris during the French Revolution in A Tale of Two Cities. The Russian composer, Tchaikovsky, composed the 1812 Overture to commemorate the Russian army's defense of the motherland against Napoleon's invading army. Fireworks displays in America would lack drama without the accompaniment of that piece of music. Lack of government funding for the arts in school or for public performances diminishes the ability to identify with the struggles that all humans have faced.

Funding the arts during challenging economic times today can help people meet their basic needs. A theater production requires many people to fill all of the jobs necessary to bring the project to fruition. In addition to actors, a play requires people to construct sets, provide lighting, sew costumes, and apply makeup. Someone must sell tickets, and others need to clean the theater each evening. Funding an orchestra provides work for dozens of musicians. When all of these individuals earn paychecks, they can provide food, shelter, and clothing for themselves.

Knowledge of the human brain informs us of the connection between music and learning. Students who have had music lessons consistently perform better on standardized tests and get higher grades in math courses. Music also has health benefits. Music and dance therapy are used in combination to help stroke victims regain or improve movement. People with autism also receive benefits from music therapy. Failure to fund the arts on an institutional level can reduce the ability of individuals to achieve their full potentials.

I recently visited the Detroit Institute of Art which is home to an impressive Diego Rivera mural which covers four walls of a large room and depicts scenes from the auto industry, the foundation of the greatness Detroit once experienced. Since then, Detroit has declared bankruptcy, and one suggestion to ameliorate its financial burden is to sell the great works of art housed at the DIA. In the short term, the idea may seem to have merit, but removing access to symbols of the city's culture along with representations from other cultures and periods of history may only further impoverish this once-great city.

Monetary considerations cannot stand alone when considering the value of a country's artistic tradition. Making the connection between funding the arts and unemployment and hunger may be a stretch. To assume that canceling the funding will alleviate or eliminate unemployment and hunger in a country arises from a misunderstanding of abstract benefits versus concrete ones. A country's aesthetic health is as important as its physical well being.

Suspending government funding for any program is fraught with risk and may put the existence of the program in limbo for an extended period of time or eliminate it altogether. The funding that was once earmarked for the arts may be impossible to retrieve from other programs to which it has been diverted.

Issue Task 19

Claim: Many problems of modern society cannot be solved by laws and the legal system.

Reason: Laws cannot change what is in people's hearts or minds.

Write a response in which you discuss the extent to which you agree or disagree with the claim and the reason on which that claim is based.

Strategies

Combine the claim and the reason into one statement using a subordinate clause.

In other words:

Because laws cannot change what is in people's hearts or minds, many problems of modern society cannot be solved by laws and the legal system.

What are the assumptions stated or implied in the claim and reason? These will provide evidence that you can refute or affirm in your argument.

a) Changing what is in people's minds and hearts will solve problems of modern society.

b) Many of modern society's problems are not rooted in illegal actions.

c) The problems of modern society are more troublesome than those of the past.

d) People will follow their hearts rather than the laws.

Opposing viewpoint:

Claim: Many problems of modern society can be solved by laws and the legal system.

Reason: Laws can override what is in people's hearts or minds.

What are the assumptions stated or implied in the claim and reason? These will provide evidence that you can refute or affirm in your argument.

a) The legal system is an effective agent of change.

b) People's minds and hearts need not be changed to be subject to laws.

c) The law has more authority than people's minds and hearts.

Alternative viewpoint:

Claim: Many problems of modern society can be solved by laws and the legal system.

Reason: People can use what is in their minds and hearts to create or change laws.

What are the assumptions stated or implied in the claim and reason?

a) People can change laws that are not effective.

Sample Essay

Society must have laws. When nomadic peoples began living together in communal groups, the need arose for rules. Individuals could not steal from the group, kill other members of the group, or be dishonest. The great religions of the world created lists of prohibited actions, calling the commission of them sins against god. Christians have the Ten Commandments, and the laws in Christian countries reflect the prohibitions in those commandments. Because most people respect and obey the laws, the legal system can solve most problems of modern society.

When the problems of modern society are the result of people's attitudes or prejudices, laws are not effective in the short term, but evidence exists that they eventually create more just conditions for everyone. Just recently, the United States commemorated the fiftieth anniversary of Martin Luther King's I Have a Dream speech during the March on Washington. This action to protest unequal treatment of minorities eventually led to President Johnson's signing the Civil Rights Act. Despite this legislation, the hearts and minds of white Americans, particularly in the South, remained unchanged for decades. However, a recent survey revealed that 72% of Americans believe that progress has been made. The fact that voters elected a black man to serve as President of the United States is the most obvious example of that progress. The bias against women in leadership roles has changed, initially as a result of the passage of the Nineteenth Amendment that allowed them to vote. Decades later, laws made it possible for women to attend college at traditionally male institutions like Harvard, Yale, and military service academies. People's hearts and minds have changed sufficiently to make it acceptable for women to serve on the Supreme Court and run as vice presidential candidates. They serve as CEOs of major corporations. Most recently, some states have passed laws making it legal for same-sex couples to marry. Alternative lifestyles have become more acceptable.

Laws may be unable to change what is in people's minds and hearts, but people can use what is in their minds and hearts to change laws or, even, entire governments. In the early years of America, citizens lived under English law. England treated the colonies like a cash cow; every time Britain needed to raise funds, it levied a new tax or tariff on the colonists. When the taxes and tariffs became too burdensome, the colonists eventually revolted, and, in 1776, declared their independence from England. Today, Americans, like citizens in most democratic countries, have a means to change the laws. The representatives and senators -also referred to as lawmakers- on both the state and national level create new laws or amend old ones to reflect the needs and desires of their constituents. Laws have been changed to reflect what people think and feel. Not so long ago, it was against the law for people of different races to marry, but now it is common to see legally married couples who are of different races. Obtaining a divorce was virtually impossible, compelling couples to remain married long after they had stopped loving each other. Women were forced to remain in abusive marriages. Due to changes in those laws, people can follow their hearts and legally remove themselves from loveless relationships.

Laws may be an effective deterrent to crime. Fear of legal consequences certainly prevents most people from acting on feelings of anger or revenge. Would-be criminals are likely to avoid a life of crime if they know they will spend time in jail or be required to pay a hefty fine. The law may not change what is in a man's heart or mind, but it can change his course of action.

Issue Task 20

The primary goal of technological advancement should be to increase people's efficiency so that they have more leisure time.

Write a response in which you discuss the extent to which you agree or disagree with the statement and explain your reasoning for the position you take. In developing and supporting your position, you should consider ways in which the statement might or might not hold true and explain how these considerations shape your position.

Strategies

Restate the issue, perhaps by reversing the order of the sentence components.

In other words:

Increasing people's efficiency so that they have more leisure time should be the primary goal of technological advancement.

Determine what question is being answered by the statement. This will help you begin to think how you would answer it and whether or not you agree with the original statement.

Why should the primary goal of technological advancement be to increase people's efficiency?

What benefits would result from technological advancement's increasing people's efficiency?

Parts of the original statement that provide evidence that you can affirm or refute.

a) **primary goal** - in other words, the first objective or the most important goal. This goal takes precedence over all others. It should be accomplished first.

b) **technological advancement -** improved uses of technology. This could include greater speed or accuracy or new uses.

c) **should be -** not exactly a mandate, more of a strong suggestion

d) **increase people's efficiency -** implies greater speed and/or fewer errors

e) **so that they have more leisure time -** time to relax, travel, pursue a hobby, etc.

Next, create a statement that expresses the opposing viewpoint, using language similar to that of the original statement.

Opposing viewpoint:

The primary goal of technological advancement should not be to increase people's efficiency so that they have more leisure time.

Increasing people's efficiency so that they have more leisure time should not be the primary goal of technological advancement.

Identify the parts of the opposing statement that provide evidence to refute or affirm.

a) **not** - either the goal of technological advancement should be something other than increased efficiency or increased efficiency should result in something other than more leisure time.

Is there any other way to look at this issue? Can you qualify the original statement in some other way? Is it possible to partially agree with the statement?

Alternative viewpoint:

One goal of technological advancement should be increasing people's efficiency so that they have more leisure time.

a) **one** - implies that other goals of technological advancement are also important

Sample Essay

To presume that technological advancements should serve the desires of humans for leisure is, at the very least, self-serving. Greater efficiency should make it possible for humans to accomplish more in a given period of time, However, advances in technology should improve not only the lives of humans in a variety of ways but also other life forms and the Earth itself. If any aspect of daily life on the planet is ignored by improvements in technology, some other aspect will suffer.

The advent of mechanization in the nineteenth century undoubtedly improved the efficiency of human activity. The cotton gin and the McCormack reaper changed agriculture forever by replacing backbreaking human labor with machine power. These advances enabled farmers to plant more crops and accomplish more work in less time. The steam engine enabled people to travel more quickly along the length of America's great rivers and across the country by train. Because more goods could move more efficiently, new factories arose and the demand for raw materials increased. Rather than creating more leisure time, mechanization created more jobs and a boost to the economies in countries that adopted it. In the twentieth century, mechanization entered the home, making it possible for housewives to complete household chores with greater efficiency. The vacuum cleaner eliminated the need to beat rugs hanging on a line in the backyard. The automatic washing machine replaced washboards and hand wringing of wet clothes. Eventually, the dishwasher and microwave would make short shrift of other kitchen chores. The upshot of these advances in technology had an effect contrary to creating more leisure time. Instead, women were able to enter the workforce. Greater efficiency in the home made possible the foray of housewives into the world of education, medicine, and business. Efficiency created by technological advances created time to complete more tasks rather than creating more leisure time.

Leisure time is not important when other aspects of life have not been improved by technological advances. The ability to spend leisure time traveling, for example, would have fewer benefits if all forms of travel had not been made safer. The frequency with which airliners crash and scores of people are killed has greatly diminished despite the fact that more planes and people take to the air every day. Going on vacation in the family car is safer because of air bags that make it more likely for passengers to survive a crash. Thanks to advances in communication technology, families can spend their leisure time enjoying any type of entertainment on their high- definition televisions.

More leisure time would be meaningless if technology had not made it possible to live longer, healthier lives. Implantable pacemakers and defibrillators enable people with heart disease to pursue active lifestyles. Those who previously were affected by debilitating osteoarthritis can have damaged joints replaced and enjoy their leisure time pain free. More children live to become healthy adults as a result of advances in vaccinations and treatment of childhood cancers.

Advances in technology have allowed scientists to monitor the climate conditions on Earth. We know that human activity has contributed to the depletion of natural resources that affect the environment. The hole in the ozone layer caused by greenhouse gases has created an alarming increase in the incidence of skin cancer. Deforestation in the rain forests has led to the extinction of important plant and animal species. Climate change is melting the ice caps, imperiling the existence of polar bears and causing water levels to rise in coastal areas. Technological advances must address these conditions, or human leisure time will become meaningless.

Issue Task 21

Unfortunately, in contemporary society, creating an appealing image has become more important than the reality or truth behind that image.

Write a response in which you discuss the extent to which you agree or disagree with the statement and explain your reasoning for the position you take. In developing and supporting your position, you should consider ways in which the statement might or might not hold true and explain how these considerations shape your position.

Strategies

Restate the issue, perhaps by reversing the order of the sentence components.

In other words:

The reality or truth behind an image has become less important in today's society than creating an appealing image.

Determine what question is being answered by the statement. This will help you begin to think how you would answer it and whether or not you agree with the original statement.

Is creating an appealing image more important than the reality behind the image in contemporary society?

Parts of the original statement that provide evidence that you can affirm or refute.

a) **Unfortunately** - implies that the statement reveals a negative consequence

b) **contemporary society** - in the present time

c) **creating** - involves some action on the part of the person desiring an image

d) **appealing image** - It goes without saying that one would want an image that appeals to others

e) **has become more important** - The need for an appealing image has grown.

f) **reality or truth behind the image** - The image is false and does not portray the real character of the individual.

Next, create a statement that expresses the opposing viewpoint, using language similar to that of the original statement.

Opposing viewpoint:

In contemporary society, creating an appealing image has not become more important than the reality or truth behind that image.

Identify the parts of the opposing statement that provide evidence to refute or affirm.

a) **has not become more important** - The image and the reality are the same.

Is there any other way to look at this issue? Can you qualify the original statement in some way? Is it possible to partially agree with the statement?

Alternative viewpoint:

In contemporary society, maintaining an appealing image has become more difficult because the reality behind that image can be more easily exposed.

Identify the parts of the alternative statement that provide evidence to refute or affirm.

a) **Maintaining** – keeping up an image over time

b) **More easily exposed** – social media broadcasts every mistake in an instant

Sample Essay

Image is everything. Canon used this tag line in an advertising campaign in the 1990's featuring tennis great, Andre Agassi who changed the look of professional tennis with his long hair and unconventional clothing on the court. Fortunately for Canon and the tennis world, Agassi had the game to support his image. He is still considered one of the greatest to play the game. In contrast, Paris Hilton, who starred in The Simple Life with friend Nichole Ritchie, has become known as a celebutante or "famous for being famous". Lacking any real talent, she has parlayed her inherited wealth into endorsing products that she has not created. For Ms Hilton, image isn't everything, it's the only thing. It is unfortunate that celebrities, athletes, and even giant corporations have created images that are contrary to the reality behind their facades.

Many athletes have gone beyond the boundaries of health and ethics to create images that elevated them to the pinnacle of their individual sports and made them very wealthy. Perhaps no one in the twenty-first century has fallen more catastrophically than Lance Armstrong. A cancer survivor, Armstrong won seven consecutive Tour de France races, the most difficult biking competition in the world. Millions of people adorned their wrists with the yellow bracelet imprinted with the Livestrong logo in support of Armstrong's cancer foundation. Just this year, the world watched as Lance Armstrong confessed in an interview with Oprah Winfrey that he was guilty of doping. He has been stripped of his titles and banned for life from professional cycling. It is fair to say that Armstrong was more concerned with his image than with the truth behind that image. Other athletes whose images have been tarnished by accusations of drug use include Roger Clemens, one of MLB's greatest pitchers, and Alex Rodriguez, whose career with the Yankees will likely end on a sour note.

The corporate world is not immune to the need for a positive image or concealing the truth behind that image. Wal-Mart has parlayed its image of lower prices all the time into becoming the world's largest retailer. Television commercials show smiling, friendly employees touting the benefits of shopping for all of your needs at Wal-Mart. When the corporation is planning a new store in a small town somewhere in America, it holds seminars for local businesses in which they reveal how these small businesses can survive and thrive after the new Wal-Mart store opens. The image is one of cooperation. The truth behind the image is that many of those small stores will close in just a few years because they cannot compete with Wal-Mart's low prices. An additional truth is that Wal-Mart is a large recipient of corporate welfare. Their image as a great place to work belies the truth that great numbers of Wal-Mart workers need public assistance to satisfy their basic needs.

Money is the biggest motivation for cultivating an image intended to mask the truth about an industry, a business, a star athlete, or a celebrity. In the 1950's, Rock Hudson was a tall, dark, and handsome leading man in some of the most popular movies made in that decade. He was also a homosexual. Although some in the movie industry suspected this, the studio that employed Hudson took measures to cover up the knowledge for many years, going as far as arranging his marriage to a woman. Those outside of the studio's top executives continued to adore Rock Hudson, and box office receipts for his movies continued to be high. When the truth about Mr. Hudson came out in the 1980's, he was dying of AIDS. Pictures showing his gaunt face and ravaged body replaced the image so carefully cultivated over several decades.

It is unfortunate that, today, image has become more important than the truth behind it. We have been told that the truth shall set you free and that if you always tell the truth, you don't have to remember what you have said to others. Those who attempt to conceal the truth - athletes, celebrities, giant corporations - must spend an inordinate amount of time and energy remembering which lies or half truths they told and to whom they told them. It is additionally unfortunate that the general public must bear some of the responsibility for these false images. People's desire for bigger, better, faster, and cheaper have driven the fabrication of these images in the pursuit of fame and fortune on the parts of the famous and popular.

Issue Task 22

Claim: The surest indicator of a great nation must be the achievements of its rulers, artists, or scientists.

Reason: Great achievements by a nation's rulers, artists, or scientists will ensure a good life for the majority of that nation's people.

Write a response in which you discuss the extent to which you agree or disagree with the claim and the reason on which that claim is based.

Strategies

Combine the claim and the reason into one statement using a subordinate clause

In other words:

Because they will ensure a good life for the majority of a nation's people, the achievements of its rulers, artists, or rulers must be the surest indicator of a great nation.

What are the assumptions stated or implied in the claim and reason? These will provide evidence that you can refute or affirm in your argument.

a) A nation's greatness is predicated on achievements in leadership, art, and science.

b) When a country's leaders, artists, and scientists are successful, the rest of the people in the country benefit.

c) Accomplishments of other groups - educators, business leaders, engineers - have little effect on the well being of society.

Opposing viewpoint:

Claim: The achievements of its rulers, artists, and scientists are not the surest indicators of a nation's greatness.

Reason: Great achievements by a nation's leaders, artists and scientists do not ensure a good life for the majority of its citizens.

What are the assumptions stated or implied in the claim and reason? These will provide evidence that you can refute or affirm in your argument.

a) Things other than the achievements of a nation's rulers, artists, and scientists determine the greatness of that nation.

Sample Essay

Rulers of a country can create conditions that make it possible for citizens to enjoy a good life. Artists can create masterpieces that generate admiration for the society that provides a home for them. Scientists can improve the lives of the citizens in the country where they live. What motivates rulers, artists and scientists determines the results of their efforts, and they can elevate their citizens or create undesirable conditions for them.

When President Johnson declared a war on poverty in the 1960's, he created Job Corps and the Headstart program. Nearly fifty years later, both institutions continue to provide opportunities for success to underprivileged young people in America. Job Corps creates a pathway to high school graduation and vocational training for youth who have failed in traditional settings. Head Start prepares very young children to enter kindergarten with the necessary skills to succeed socially and academically. The longevity of these programs is a result of their proven ability to create better lives for at-risk young people in our society.

Scientists in many fields have improved the lives of humans around the world. Medical advances have not only delivered cures for many cancers and other deadly diseases but made the treatment of them less debilitating. Some former killers, like smallpox and polio, have been virtually eliminated. Other scientists have developed cleaner fuels for the motors that make us mobile and keep us warm or cool in our homes. A majority of citizens benefit from breathing cleaner air and suffering fewer respiratory ailments.

The achievements of a country's artists may be an indication of its greatness but may have little to do with creating a good life for a majority of its citizens. One can see the great works of the Renaissance in Italy and conclude that the atmosphere of the fifteenth century supported the efforts of artistic giants like da Vinci and Michelangelo. Without wealthy patrons or the support of the Vatican, however, many Italian greats might have labored in obscurity, struggling to obtain materials or even feed and clothe themselves. The artistic achievements do not reflect the conditions under which most Italians at the time lived. Ordinary citizens accrued no benefit from the accomplishments of great painters, sculptors or composers.

Likewise, the achievements of the leaders and scientists in Nazi Germany during the 1930's and 40's did not indicate the greatness of that nation. It did not take long for the other countries of Europe to uncover Hitler's motivation for assuming power and invading neighboring countries. Attempting to eradicate entire groups of people does not speak to a leader's ability to engender loyalty and trust in his countrymen. Additionally, Hitler encouraged the perverted medical experiments conducted by Dr. Mengele on inmates of the concentration camps. Hitler's monomaniacal behavior eventually led to Germany's defeat in WWII.

Areas of achievement omitted in the claim include business and education. Without great achievements in education, prospective leaders, artists, and scientists may never have gained the opportunity to reach their potentials. The access to free, public education for all of its citizens has had the greatest impact on their ability to ensure a good life for themselves and their families. Many leaders, artists, and scientists would likely acknowledge the fact that they discovered their love of politics, painting, or biology in a classroom.

Achievements in the business arena also contribute the well being of a nation's citizens. The ability of the United States to insure the safety of its citizens during wartime arose in large part from manufacturing concerns that procured raw materials and fashioned warships, fighter planes, and munitions. Giant retailers hire tens of thousands of sales associates to help them provide all manner of goods to the general public. Their paychecks help these workers provide for their families' welfare.

The achievements of leaders, artists, scientists, educators and others cannot contribute to a country's greatness unless those achievements ensure better lives for the citizens of that country. When their achievements ignore the basic tenets of humanity, the citizens of their societies will suffer.

Issue Task 23

Claim: Researchers should not limit their investigations to only those areas in which they expect to discover something that has an immediate, practical application.

Reason: It is impossible to predict the outcome of a line of research with any certainty.

Write a response in which you discuss the extent to which you agree or disagree with the claim and the reason on which that claim is based.

Strategies

Restate the Claim:

Combine the claim and reason into one statement using a subordinate clause.

In other words:

Because it is impossible to predict the outcome of a line of research with any certainty, researchers should not limit their investigations to only those areas in which they expect to discover something that has an immediate, practical application.

What are the assumptions in the claim and reason? These will be statements that you can either refute or affirm.

Assumption 1: All research is valuable.

Assumption 2: The outcome of research is unpredictable.

Assumption 3: Research for research's sake has value.

Assumption 4: Research need not have practical, applicable results.

Opposing viewpoint:

Claim - Researchers should limit their investigations to only those areas in which they expect to discover something that has an immediate, practical application.

Reason: The cost of research is prohibitive.

What are the assumptions in the claim and reason? These will be statements that you can either refute or affirm.

Assumption 1: Not all research is valuable.

Assumption 2: Researchers must be practical.

Assumption 3: Research is too costly to conduct without a practical outcome.

Assumption 4: The goal of research should be financial reward.

Sample Essay

Research is investigation that leads to discovery. Researchers are like the early explorers who set out to find new worlds. Even though the goals of those explorers might have been to discover gold or spices or other valuable resources, there was no guarantee that they would find what they sought. Kings and queens spared no expense as they outfitted sailing vessels whose voyages might or might not return with untold riches. Those sailors faced unknown dangers and the vagaries of winds and water in order to claim new territories for their sovereigns. Centuries later, there is very little left of a material nature to discover on Earth. Exploration now takes place in outer space and in laboratories. Should all of these endeavors require practical and immediate results?

It has been nearly fifty years since US President John F. Kennedy promised that the United States would land a man on the moon before the end of that decade. At the time, the only goal that seemed evident was to surpass the Soviet Union in the space race. What possible practical applications could result from that? The focus was on creating rockets powerful enough to propel a spacecraft outside of the earth's atmosphere and a capsule that would insure the safety of its occupants. Scientists needed to create meals that could be dehydrated in order to fit the confines of the capsule. Numerous safety issues had to be addressed. As it turns out, many of the innovations developed for space travel did have practical uses for the general population. Space blankets come to mind. With an appearance similar to that of a piece of tinfoil, space blankets have become standard items in emergency kits because they can be folded into a very small square but have sufficient ability to keep someone warm who might be stranded on a highway in cold weather.

Men of a certain age around the world are thankful for the accidental application of a medication originally designed to treat heart disease. Without this medical research, the world would not have Viagra. Other conveniences are the result of mistakes made in the laboratory. Most practical among them are White Out, a liquid paper used for correcting typing or writing errors, and stick notes. A children's toy that used to be very popular is Silly Putty, another scientific flub. It came in a plastic egg and could be used to lift comic strips from a paper medium. Although some of these have had no real redeeming effect on mankind, they were commercial successes.

There is no debate about the cost of research. Setting up the environment in which research must take place involves expensive construction materials and specifications, proper equipment, and appropriately educated scientists to carry on the work. The work itself can be painstaking and long. Important discoveries are rarely made overnight. Spain's Ferdinand and Isabela probably complained about the cost of Christopher Columbus' journery across the ocean, and the returns were slight, but imagine what the world would be like today if they hadn't risked so much. The New World, itself, was an accidental discovery. Columbus bumped into it while seeking a shorter route to the Far East. If research is limited to investigations that will only lead to practical applications, other new worlds may be overlooked or missed entirely.

Issue Task 24

Educational institutions should actively encourage their students to choose fields of study that will prepare them for lucrative careers.

Write a response in which you discuss your views on the policy and explain your reasoning for the position you take. In developing and supporting your position, you should consider the possible consequences of implementing the policy and explain how these consequences shape your position.

Strategies

Restate the issue, perhaps by reversing the order of the sentence components.

In other words:

To prepare their students for lucrative careers, educational institutions should actively encourage their students

Determine what question is being answered by the statement. This will help you begin to think how you would answer it and whether or not you agree with the original statement.

Which fields of study should educational institutions actively encourage their students to choose?

Parts of the original statement that provide evidence that you can affirm or refute.

a) **Educational institutions -** Does this include technical schools, education one may receive in the military, etc?

b) **actively encourage -** implies promoting through direct contact with students, advertising, etc.

Next, create a statement that expresses the opposing viewpoint, using language similar to that of the original statement."

Opposing viewpoint:

Educational institutions should actively encourage their students to choose fields of study that will prepare them for careers that are in high demand.

Educational institutions should not actively encourage their students to choose fields of study that prepare them for only lucrative careers.

Parts of the opposing statement that provide evidence that you can affirm or refute

a) high demand – more jobs available increases the likelihood of finding work

Is there any other way to look at this issue? Can you qualify the original statement in some way? Is it possible to partially agree with the statement?

Alternative viewpoint:

Overlooking less lucrative careers will create lack of practitioners in other vital areas.

Parts of the alternative statement that provide evidence that you can affirm or refute.

a) create a lack – there will not be people seeking jobs that are not lucrative

b) vital – jobs that are necessary to provide safety

Sample Essay

The job market is highly competitive. Many college graduates have failed to find work in their chosen careers, and many have even returned home to live with their parents. The demand for practitioners in some careers has risen while the demand for others has fallen. Presuming that students who study for jobs in lucrative careers will have more luck finding employment may be shortsighted. Considering the vagaries of today's workplace, students should pursue courses of study for careers they will find rewarding in ways other than just financially.

Literature is replete with tales that warn us of the dire consequences attached to the pursuit of money. Charles Dickens gave us the character, Ebenezer Scrooge, as a morality lesson to demonstrate how focusing on the acquisition of wealth leads to loneliness and bitterness. In Greek mythology, one finds King Midas who was able to turn everything he touched to gold. His downfall came when he touched his beloved daughter, also turning her to a lifeless statue made of gold. Readers of such tales are meant to infer that relationships are more important than any amount of money.

It has been said, "Do what you love, and the money will follow." Choosing a career one loves will make it easy to go to work each day. A small business owner who sells a product he loves will convey that affection to his customers. They will enjoy shopping with him and recommend his store to their friends and family. As his customer base expands, he will sell more products and make more money. In contrast, the shop owner who works only for the money may resent spending his days doing something he doesn't enjoy, and his attitude may be reflected in his treatment of customers. His pursuit of money alone may lead to the opposite result as his customers desert him for more pleasant experiences elsewhere.

Over time, demand for practitioners in various careers ebbs and wanes. At one time, teachers were in short supply, so high school graduates went to college to become teachers. In a short span of time, there was a surplus of newly-minted educators, many of whom could not find jobs in their chosen careers. The practice of law promises great financial rewards. More people have trained for that route to riches than there are positions to be filled, and many lawyers now occupy places in graduate schools to learn a new skill.

Adopting this policy not only leads to a glut of people trained for lucrative careers but leads to a shortage of people trained to fill lower-paying but, nonetheless, important positions. If people seek only lucrative jobs, institutions will lack custodians to clean and maintain their facilities. Small-town police and fire departments will lack sufficient personnel to ensure the safety of their communities.

Following a career path for any reason other than love of the work involved with it will certainly lead to dissatisfaction and unhappiness. The young woman who wants nothing more than to dance all day long will be happier working for union scale in a dance troupe than seeking a management position in a bank.

Just yesterday, Pope Francis repeated the biblical warning; the love of money is the root of all evil. Encouraging students to seek only money rather than intangible rewards leads to the downfall of individuals or large groups of people. The Ponzi scheme created by Bernie Madoff is a prime example. He convinced people to invest their life savings in his company which was nothing but a house of cards. When it collapsed, ordinary people lost everything, Madoff, himself, went to prison, and his son committed suicide.

In order to function, the world needs people to fill a wide variety of jobs. Not all are lucrative, but they ensure the safety of the world's citizens by protecting them from crime, disease, and disasters. These occupations produce rewards that cannot be purchased with any amount of money.

Issue Task 25

> *Claim: Major policy decisions should always be left to politicians and other government experts.*
>
> *Reason: Politicians and other government experts are more informed and thus have better judgment and perspective than do members of the general public.*
>
> *Write a response in which you discuss the extent to which you agree or disagree with the claim and the reason on which that claim is based.*

Strategies

Combine the claim and the reason into one statement using a subordinate clause.

In other words:

Because politicians and other government experts are more informed and thus have better judgment and perspective than do members of the general public, they alone should make major policy decisions.

What are the assumptions stated or implied in the claim and reason? These will provide evidence that you can refute or affirm in your argument.

a) Major policy decisions occur only at the government level.

b) People other than politicians and government experts are not well informed enough to make major policy decisions.

c) No groups other than government experts or the general public are likely to make policy decisions.

Opposing viewpoint:

Claim: Major policy decisions should not always be left to politicians and other government experts.

Reason: Politicians and other government experts are no better informed or have better judgment and perspective than do members of the general public.

What are the assumptions stated or implied in the claim and reason? These will provide evidence that you can refute or affirm in your argument.

a) People other than politicians and government experts are capable of making major policy decisions.

Sample Essay

Major policy decisions guide the actions of people in virtually all walks of life. The Federal Reserve determines policy regarding interest rates that banks charge their biggest customers and, consequently, the interest rates that the average consumer pays for mortgages and auto loans. Although the Fed chairman is appointed by the President, he or she must have autonomy to make monetary decisions independently of politicians. Certainly, the average citizen lacks the specific knowledge necessary to create fiscal policy for the entire country. However, many policies that guide the lives of Americans today would not exist were it not for activism on the parts of ordinary citizens. When policy decisions affect the basic rights of humans, the contributions of the general public cannot be overlooked.

Politicians do not always display better judgment than the general public when they make or uphold policy. For generations, states in the South enforced laws arising from the policy of segregation. Black Americans were banned from eating in white restaurants, using white restrooms, or attending white schools. In 1892, Homer Plessy, in an act that foreshadowed Rosa Parks' behavior on a Montgomery bus in 1951, sat in a designated "white" car of the East Louisiana Railroad. After Plessy identified himself as a black man, authorities arrested him. Plessy's case went all the way to the Supreme Court, where, in 1896, all but one justice declared that the policy of separate but equal facilities for white and black people was acceptable and did not violate the Fourteenth Amendment. The facilities for black people never reached the equal level of those for white people. Their schools were inferior; the buildings were run down, and the books were discarded by white schools. For decades, black children were banned from riding school buses and, often, had to walk long distances to attend schools designated for them. Nearly half a decade after the Plessy case, the NAACP sponsored a case in Topeka, Kansas, that represented several parents who wanted their children to be allowed to attend schools in their neighborhoods rather than the "separate but equal" schools. In a unanimous decision in 1954, the Supreme Court in Brown v the Board of Education of Topeka, Kansas, ruled that the separate but equal policy was unconstitutional, thereby integrating public schools throughout the country. Left to their own devices, politicians and other government experts would have continued to allow de facto segregation in the United States. Without the impetus from those suffering under the policy, little change would have occurred or would have come much later.

When a policy has been in effect for a long time, it becomes difficult to change. Even though the Supreme Court decision of 1954 prohibited segregation, people in the South were reluctant to grant civil rights to their black neighbors. They held onto their belief in the superiority of the white man, a remnant of the days of slavery on southern plantations. Their leaders devised requirements for voting that made it virtually impossible for black men and women to exercise their right of suffrage. When any group of citizens cannot vote to change policy or elect legislators who represent their interests, repressive laws and regulations persist. Without the efforts of the NAACP, the Freedom Riders, student activists from northern universities and the leadership of Martin Luther King, Jr, President Lyndon B. Johnson may not have been convinced to sign into law the Civil Rights Act of 1964.

One should not assume that politicians and government experts are better informed than the general public and, therefore, the only ones capable of making or changing major policy decisions. Senators, representative, and the president all select advisers from the general public. They look for the best and brightest in a variety of fields to fill positions in their offices and the cabinet. The expertise they gained while plying their trades in the public sector makes them valuable assets at the national level. Although average citizens do not have the power to create policy, their voices contribute to the choices those politicians and government experts make to change the manner in which the business of everyday life is carried out.

Issue Task 26

It is more harmful to compromise one's own beliefs than to adhere to them.

Write a response in which you discuss the extent to which you agree or disagree with the statement and explain your reasoning for the position you take. In developing and supporting your position, you should consider ways in which the statement might or might not hold true and explain how these considerations shape your position.

Strategies

Restate the issue, perhaps by reversing the order of the sentence components.

In other words:

Adhering to one's own beliefs is less harmful than compromising them.

Determine what question is being answered by the statement. This will help you begin to think how you would answer it and whether or not you agree with the original statement.

Is it more harmful to compromise one's own beliefs than to adhere to them?

Parts of the original statement that provide evidence that you can affirm or refute.

a) more harmful- expresses a degree of harm

b) compromise- give and take

c) one's own beliefs - tenets or opinions

d) adhere - stick to

Next, create a statement that expresses the opposing viewpoint, using language similar to that of the original statement.

Opposing viewpoint:

It is more harmful to adhere to one's own beliefs than to compromise them.

It is more harmful to adhere to one's beliefs than to compromise them.

Parts of the opposing statement that provide evidence that you can affirm or refute.

Evidence is the same as in the original statement.

Is there any other way to look at this issue? Can you qualify the original statement in some way? Is it possible to partially agree with the statement?

Alternative viewpoint:

Depending on the circumstances, it is as harmful to adhere to one's own beliefs as it is to compromise them.

Parts of the alternative statement that provide evidence that you can affirm or refute.

a) Depending on the circumstances – allows both choices to be correct

Sample Essay

The nineteenth century transcendentalist writer, Ralph Waldo Emerson, wrote that a foolish consistency is the hobgoblin of little minds. Adhering to one's own beliefs can result in a stubborn refusal to consider other points of view. Ignoring or denigrating the beliefs of others, can lead to persecuting individuals or entire groups of people. On the other hand, compromising can lead to a watered-down version of a plan or goal, leaving both sides in a conflict unsatisfied. Depending on the situation, either steadfastness regarding one's beliefs or reaching a compromise may be the correct action.

In Germany during the 1930's, Adolph Hitler rose to power and began to invade neighboring countries in an effort to establish the supremacy of the Aryan race. His unshakable belief that those with Aryan blood were superior to all other races led to the systematic roundup and murder of other groups including Jews, gypsies, homosexuals, and the mentally defective in concentration camps. Hitler's beliefs were so entrenched and his rhetoric so impassioned that he created a legion of followers who carried out his orders. His refusal to compromise his beliefs led to his conquering many countries in central Europe and, ultimately, to his demise.

On a much smaller scale, the actions of the city council in my hometown have created an impasse between city management and local businesses. The council has devised a plan to alleviate a budget deficit for the coming year, reduce expenditures for years to come, and add properties to the tax rolls. It put up for sale by bid all of the municipally-owned parking lots in the downtown area. The building and business owners downtown did not know of the plan until the list of properties appeared in the local newspaper. In a special city council meeting, the mayor admitted that the council assumed that the building owners would purchase the lots abutting their buildings. At least two of the lots are protected by the urban renewal plan from the late 1960's, so they were removed from the list. The building owners fronted by the other lots spoke about the inadvisability of selling them, citing the complexity of both buying and maintaining lots shared by multiple owners. Determined to reduce the city's responsibility for the lots, the mayor devised a new plan that requires people who park downtown for the entire workday to purchase annual parking permits. Again, building and business owners spoke to the council about the financial hardship that the new plan would put on workers downtown and the logistics of allocating spaces to preserve access to retail businesses. The issue has consumed way too much time and energy for the small savings that the city would see. In fact, the city's hiring someone to enforce parking regulations would offset the savings. Each side is more concerned about being right than understanding the other's point of view. Adhering to one's point of view, in this case, prevents further progress in solving the city's budget issues and creates resentment from business owners toward the council.

Adhering to one's beliefs is essential when attempting to redress wrongs committed against humanity.

America today would be a very different place had Martin Luther King, Jr compromised his belief that all men, regardless of color, were entitled to the same rights and freedoms. When he spoke on the steps of the Lincoln Memorial in Washington, DC, fifty years ago, he did not proclaim that only some black men should be treated with equality or that only members of some religions should be treated with equality, but that black men and white men, Jews and Gentiles, Protestants and Catholics all should be granted the same freedoms guaranteed in the Constitution. In the same manner, Gandhi also adhered to his belief in freedom from the oppression when he demonstrated against the British rule in India. Despite their use of peaceful protest, both King and Gandhi were assassinated for their unwillingness to compromise their beliefs. Both men knew the inherent dangers of their actions, but were not deterred from their objectives.

Although it may be painful to compromise one's beliefs, the most significant decisions in America's history are most often the result of conflicting sides' willingness to concede at least a portion of their own plan. America's founding fathers compromised to find a balance between federal and state's rights, creating the legislature we still have today. The Missouri Compromise limited the expansion of slave states in America. When compromise limits the benefits of people affected by an idea or action, it should be abandoned in favor of adhering to one's beliefs.

Issue Task 27

Claim: Colleges and universities should specify all required courses and eliminate elective courses in order to provide clear guidance for students.

Reason: College students - like people in general - prefer to follow directions rather than make their own decisions.

Write a response in which you discuss the extent to which you agree or disagree with the claim and the reason on which that claim is based.

Strategies

Combine the claim and the reason into one statement using a subordinate clause.

In other words:

Because college students prefer to follow directions rather than make their own decisions, colleges and universities should specify all required courses and eliminate elective courses in order to provide clear guidance for students.

What are the assumptions stated or implied in the claim and reason? These will provide evidence that you can refute or affirm in your argument.

a) Elective courses are not necessary to a good education.

b) People dislike making decisions.

c) Providing guidance means making decisions for others

Opposing viewpoint:

Claim: Colleges and universities should not specify all required courses and eliminate elective courses.

Reason: College students - like people in general-prefer to make their own choices rather than follow directions.

Assumptions:

a) College students are capable of choosing their own courses.

Sample Essay

If people only and always followed directions, little new would ever be discovered. To presume that college students can succeed only when their courses are carefully proscribed diminishes the ability of young adults to make wise choices. Students may willingly accept some direction in their choice of courses but don't necessarily want to follow directions. Those who choose their own path may be more satisfied. Those who provide guidance usually make suggestions and allow those whom they are guiding to make their own choices.

Most high-school students, especially in small towns, have little choice in selecting courses. State departments of education and local administrators establish guidelines for graduation requirements which generally include a specific number of credits in English, social studies, science, and math. Electives are rare. Students are apt to relish the opportunity to take some elective courses in college. In doing so they may discover areas of interest in disciplines they didn't even know existed or discover strengths and talents they didn't know they had.

I have two sisters who exemplify the opposite extremes of choice. In the fall of each of our senior years in high school, we traveled for several days with our mother to visit colleges we were interested in attending. Despite being raised in the same house by the same parents, each of us had different interests and personalities, so each of our trips included a variety of colleges. My mother and my older sister embarked on their journey, schedule of visits and interviews in hand. They went to the campuses of large universities, business schools, and small private colleges. Each had something to recommend it until they visited a small school in western Massachusetts. My sister rejected it out-of-hand because it had too little structure. There were no required courses: students were free to enroll in any class they desired. She eventually selected an all-women's college that was fairly liberal but did have required core courses for the first two years. A few years later, my younger sister took the trip with Mom. Eventually, she, too, settled on an all-women's college, but one that had only one requirement, a single semester of a writing-intensive course. She explored a variety of courses and took some unorthodox electives. She discovered a discipline that she wanted to pursue, and, after two years, transferred to a large state university in the Midwest. If all colleges set rigid course guidelines and eliminated electives, my older sister may have been just fine, but my younger sister would likely have felt stifled and may have quit college altogether.

Limiting choices stifles creativity. A college student majoring in art, for example, may want to focus on one medium, but the college has created required courses in each medium. The art student's lack of ability to focus on sculpture as his means of expression may frustrate him to the extent that he will pack his bags and leave. In contrast, the art student may want to dabble in each medium, but he is forced by the college to choose only one, and must spend the years in college painting when he would have liked to explore sculpture or mixed media. This student, too, may leave the school. In these cases, the rigid structure of required courses may result in the college's losing population and tuition dollars

Humans want some guidance and structure in their lives. It is helpful to know when to show up for work and how long the workday will be. They like knowing what their responsibilities at work include and how to complete their tasks. However, they want to choose the type of employment and employer. Communist Russia forced people into specific occupations based on the country's need for people to accomplish certain tasks. There was virtually no unemployment. However, lack of choice led to less productivity, and communism ultimately failed. Forcing people to work at jobs they haven't chosen or college students to take courses they don't want can only lead to discontent and poor performance.

Issue Task 28

> *True success can be measured primarily in terms of the goals one sets for oneself.*
>
> *Write a response in which you discuss the extent to which you agree or disagree with the statement and explain your reasoning for the position you take. In developing and supporting your position, you should consider ways in which the statement might or might not hold true and explain how these considerations shape your position.*

Strategies

Restate the issue, perhaps by reversing the order of the sentence components.

In other words:

The goals one sets for oneself are the measures of true success.

Determine what question is being answered by the statement. This will help you begin to think how you would answer it and whether or not you agree with the original statement.

Is true success measured by the goals one sets for oneself?

Parts of the original statement that provide evidence that you can affirm or refute.

a) True success - in this case, worthy of celebration or acknowledgment

b) measured - quantified, valued

c) primarily - most important

d) goals - achievements, destinations

e) one sets for oneself - as opposed to those set for one by others

Next, create a statement that expresses the opposing viewpoint, using language similar to that of the original statement.

Opposing viewpoint:

True success is not measured primarily by the goals one sets for oneself.

Parts of the opposing statement that provide evidence that you can affirm or refute.

a) not - other measurements of success are equally or more important

Is there any other way to look at this issue? Can you qualify the original statement in some way? Is it possible to partially agree with the statement?

Alternative viewpoint:

True success is measured by the goals one achieves.

Parts of the alternative statement that provide evidence that you can affirm or refute.

a) achieves - setting goals is not a sufficient measure of success

Sample Essay

People set goals that are sometimes simple and at other times complex. Rare is the individual who hasn't created a New Year's resolution to exercise more, lose weight, or quit smoking. Rarer still is the individual who has managed to keep that resolution. As important as individual goals are, so are those set by leaders in business, science and government. When the president of a country sets goals for his term of office, he considers the welfare of all citizens. When a CEO sets a goal for his company, he hopes that achieving it will benefit his workers and shareholders. Scientists hope to improve the lives of all humans when he sets a goal to discover a treatment for a deadly disease. Small and personal or grand and universal, all goals are indications of people's seeking success.

Just yesterday morning, I watched as an IT specialist from North Carolina set off from a soccer field near my house to cross the Atlantic in a cluster balloon, a journey predicted to take from three to six days with the possibility of landing anywhere from Norway to Africa. It was like a scene from the movie Up as 365 colored, helium-filled balloons lifted Jonathan Trappe and his rubber boat silently into the air. The fantastic craft quickly disappeared into the morning mist. This same man has flown cluster balloons over the Alps and across the English Channel, but this was to be his most ambitious undertaking.. It is unfortunate that this journey ended in Newfoundland just twelve hours after it began. However, if success were to be measured by the goals one sets for himself, Mr. Trappe would, indeed, be considered successful.

It could be argued that setting goals that are easily attainable is not real success. The poet Robert Browning said, “a man's reach should exceed his grasp." Man should strive for achievements beyond his current ability. It is the only way to grow. When Christa McAuliffe was a young girl, she told a friend that she wanted to go into space someday. The opportunity arose when President Reagan made the decision to put a teacher on the space shuttle. Christa applied and saw her goal realized when she was selected to be the first teacher in space where she planned to present lessons live from the Challenger. Less than a minute after takeoff, the shuttle broke apart and McAuliffe, along with the rest of the crew, was killed. Although her mission was cut short, she has been lauded for setting a lofty goal and undergoing the rigorous training to become an astronaut. Had the Wright Brothers not set a goal of achieving manned flight in the earliest decade of the twentieth century, space travel likely would have occurred much later. Orville and Wilbur Wright could have lived out the rest of their lives building and repairing bicycles, setting and achieving the goal of customer satisfaction with their excellent workmanship. However, setting loftier goals, the Wright brothers not only achieved success for themselves but inspired generations of fliers.

Ordinary individuals set their sights on reaching significant goals as well. They want to become more fit, so they join a gym. They want to lose a few or many pounds, so they join Weight Watchers. They want to quit smoking, so they join a cessation program at their local hospital. They all begin with great resolve and enthusiasm. After a few weeks, visits to the gym become less frequent, cake and ice cream become more appealing than pounds lost, and a cigarette after dinner becomes irresistible. Some of these individuals will fail to meet their goals, but others will try again and ultimately succeed. Without setting goals in the first place, they surely would have failed.

Many who have reached outstanding levels of achievement did not succeed in reaching their goals with their first attempt. The Wright brothers built many airplanes that failed to fly. Three NASA astronauts, including Gus Grissom, died in a prelaunch test in 1967. Civil Rights workers were murdered in Mississippi. Setbacks did not stop the progress of flight, the space race, or the Civil Rights Movement. Failure is not measured by an individual’s inability to meet his or her goals. Failure is the result of giving up or not trying at all. Setting a goal is the first step on the road to success.

Issue Task 29

The effectiveness of a country's leaders is best measured by examining the well-being of that country's citizens.

Write a response in which you discuss the extent to which you agree or disagree with the statement and explain your reasoning for the position you take. In developing and supporting your position, you should consider ways in which the statement might or might not hold true and explain how these considerations shape your position.

Strategies

Restate the issue, perhaps by reversing the order of the sentence components.

In other words:

The well-being of a country's citizens is the best measure of its leaders' effectiveness.

Determine what question is being answered by the statement. This will help you begin to think how you would answer it and whether or not you agree with the original statement.

What is the best means of measuring the effectiveness of a country's leaders?

Parts of the original statement that provide evidence that you can affirm or refute.

a) Effective leaders ensure the well being of a country's citizens.

b) Other measures of a leader's effectiveness are less important than the well being of the country's citizens.

Next, create a statement that expresses the opposing viewpoint, using language similar to that of the original statement.

Opposing viewpoint:

The effectiveness of a country's leaders is not best measured by the well-being of that country's citizens.

Is there any other way to look at this issue? Can you qualify the original statement in some way? Is it possible to partially agree with the statement?

Alternative viewpoint:

The well-being of a country's citizens is one measure of its leaders' effectiveness.

Sample Essay

When history judges the effectiveness of a country's leader, it considers the decisions he or she made that led to a good life for the citizens of the country. High employment rates, accessibility to affordable health care, a good school system, a reasonable inflation rate, and security from invasion by enemies are some of those important measures. When those conditions exist for an extended period of time, the leader can be called effective, perhaps even great.

America has elected presidents who displayed great leadership in areas other than government, believing that their skills would create a sense of well being for its citizens. General Dwight D. Eisenhower, Supreme Commander of the allied troops in Europe during WWII, created the strategy for the D-Day invasion of Normandy that eventually decided the war in favor of the Allies. "I Like Ike" became the campaign slogan that helped to elect him president in 1952 and again in1956. Eisenhower's demonstrated ability to secure victory over communism and fascism in Europe made him the popular choice to lead post-war America. The prosperity of Americans during the '50's would make it reasonable to conclude that Eisenhower was an effective leader.

Perhaps no other president in the twentieth century faced more challenges during his term of leadership than Franklin Delano Roosevelt. First elected in 1932, he faced the Herculean task of lifting the country out of the Great Depression. Large numbers of Americans were unemployed, hungry, and homeless. With the blessings of Congress, FDR established the New Deal which contained programs like the CCC (Civil Conservation Corps) that provided both paying jobs for Americans and a necessary service in America's woodlands. During the first year of FDR's third term, on December 7, 1941, the Japanese attacked American ships at Pearl Harbor. As a result, American would become engaged in WWII, fighting both in Europe and the Pacific. FDR's ability to lead during wartime was exemplified by his ability to forge an alliance with the USSR, a former adversary. Americans were so convinced of this president's ability to improve the well being of all citizens that they reelected FDR for an unprecedented fourth term.

Some might argue that leaders in the twenty first century have made some decisions that were designed to secure the well being of Americans but have infringed on citizens' rights or have not had the intended consequences. After the terrorist attacks on the World Trade Center in 2001, the leaders of America declared war on Al Qaeda and vowed to hunt down those responsible for the attacks and to prevent further threats to America's safety. Patriotic fever swept the nation, and most citizens heartily approved of President Bush's decision. Twelve years later, American troops are still fighting in Iraq and Afghanistan, and the American people are weary of the protracted war. The Patriot Act was created to enable the tracking of suspected terrorists in the United States, but many citizens protested the invasion of privacy inherent in that act. Travel by air throughout the country became a more laborious undertaking with security measures implemented at every airport. Even though Americans feel safer when they travel, they feel that some freedoms have been lost. The well-being of the majority may occur at the price of individual freedom.

Just recently, the government of Syria used chemical weapons in the form of poisonous gas on its own citizens. President Obama immediately declared that the US should take military action against Syria to eliminate these chemical weapons. Should Syria continue to use chemical weapons, American troops and civilians in the Middle East may be in danger. A military strike might ensure their well being. On the other hand, Syria and its allies could retaliate, putting even more Americans in danger. Decisions about protecting the well being of Americans are often fraught with conflicting consequences; the right choice is not always obvious or easy, and leaders are subject to harsh criticism if their choices are unpopular.

Leaders of the free world do attempt to secure the well being of their citizens by maintaining a vibrant economy, protecting individual rights, and insuring their safety by eliminating threats both foreign and domestic. Many of those leaders also try to improve the lives of people who are oppressed or murdered by their own leaders in other countries. The effectiveness of any leader to secure the well-being of the citizens may not become apparent until his or her actions are viewed from a historical perspective.

Issue Task 30

In any field - business, politics, education, government - those in power should be required to step down after five years.

Write a response in which you discuss your views on the policy and explain your reasoning for the position you take. In developing and supporting your position, you should consider the possible consequences of implementing the policy and explain how these consequences shape your position.

Strategies

Restate the issue, perhaps by reversing the order of the sentence components.

In other words:

Those in power in any field - business, politics, education, government- should be required to step down after five years.

Determine what question is being answered by the statement. This will help you begin to think how you would answer it and whether or not you agree with the original statement.

When should those in power in any field be required to step down?

How long should those in power in any field be allowed to retain their positions?

Consequences of adopting this policy:

a) Fresh ideas will be introduced every five years.

b) Long- range planning becomes difficult.

c) Ineffective leaders can be replaced quickly.

Next, create a statement that expresses the opposing viewpoint, using language similar to that of the original statement.

Opposing viewpoint:

In any field – business, politics, education, government – those in power should not be required to step down after five years.

Consequences of adopting this policy:

a) More experience leads to better decisions.

b) Those in power may become complacent.

c) Long- range planning becomes possible.

Is there any other way to look at this issue? Can you qualify the original statement in some way? Is it possible to partially agree with the statement?

Alternative viewpoint:

In any field - business, politics, education, government - those in power should step down when they are no longer effective.

Consequences of adopting this policy:

a) Effective leaders can remain in power.

Sample Essay

A five-year limit on tenure in any field appears arbitrary. Some in positions of power or leadership should leave office sooner, and some should be allowed to remain for as long as they want. Examples exist on the local, state, national, and international level that support either the original or the opposing point of view. It is impossible and impractical to establish hard-and-fast rules about the length of time anyone should serve in a position of power or leadership.

America's founding fathers, in order to eliminate the potential tyranny associated with sovereigns like kings, established a democracy in which the people would elect their leaders. They also established a four-year term as president. It was not until the middle of the twentieth century that the number of terms a president could serve was limited to two. US senators and representatives serve two and six year terms respectively, and they may remain in office as long as the voters choose to keep them. The frequency with which they must seek reelection allows the voters to keep those who represent them well and eliminate those whose actions do not benefit them.

Many American presidents have served more than one term. President Franklin D. Roosevelt was elected for four consecutive terms during the most challenging period in our history. He led us out of the Great Depression by creating the New Deal replete with public works projects that provided honorable and necessary work for Americans who had lost everything. He was Commander in Chief during most of the WWII years. It would be difficult to imagine how America would have fared during those trying times if our nation's leader had been compelled to serve only 5 years. In contrast to the beneficial results of FDR's tenure, the Russians were suffering under the dictator, Stalin who did not have to run for reelection. Despite the Communist 5-year plans for productivity, millions of Russians died from starvation and persecution. Whereas Americans were well-served by FDR's lengthy leadership, Russians would have been better off if Stalin had been forced out of office.

One negative consequence of limiting the tenure of those in positions of leadership is the inability to plan long-term. In virtually any field, the leader cannot effect change without first creating a cohort of like-minded individuals. Convincing those with the same point of view to work toward the leader's goals is difficult enough without also having to persuade those on the fence or diametrically opposed to his or her ideas. This can consume a great deal of time and energy. Once the cohort is established, the members are apt to want some concessions or compromises from each other before the final objective is clearly delineated. Additional steps in the process may include conducting polls, surveys, or research. Several years can elapse during this process at the end of which, the leader may have little time remaining to fulfill his goals. If the leader is compelled to leave in the middle of the journey, the goal may never be achieved, and the new leader may have very different ideas about the needs of the institution he is directing and restart the entire complex process. In contrast, a leader who knows his time in office is limited may work more diligently to accomplish his objectives. When people have deadlines for completing tasks or assignments, they organize their time more efficiently. Imagine a student having a research project with no due date. He or she might procrastinate or never do the work at all.

Experience is the best teacher. A good leader in any field becomes more adept. He or she is apt to face similar situations over the course of his tenure and use what he has learned from past actions and consequences to inform his decision making. He will have learned what works, what doesn't, and how to negotiate for the best outcome. Longevity can also lead to stagnation, and some are inclined to do things the way they've always been done. They are resistant to change or even compromise. Because voters, company directors, and boards of education have the discretion and power to remove institutional leaders when they are no longer effective, an arbitrary term limit is not necessary. Term limits can truncate the careers of effective leaders or extend those of leaders who should have been removed soon after assuming their positions.

4

Analyze an Argument Task

In the Analyze an Argument task, you will take an approach that differs from that in the Analyze an Issue task. You will not be asked to develop and defend a point of view. You will be asked to analyze an argument and the evidence and assumptions on which it is based. You will be presented by a brief passage that makes an argument either for taking some course of action, following a recommendation, or supporting a prediction. You should read the passage carefully to identify either stated or unstated assumptions or to determine the line of reasoning used by the author of the passage. The directions will instruct you to approach your analysis in any of several ways. You may be asked to state what additional evidence is needed to make the argument sound, what questions will need to be answered before accepting a recommendation, or whether a prediction based on the argument is reasonable.

As in the Analyze an Issue task, there is no "right" answer or approach. It is important to stay on topic, use sound reasoning and examples in your response, and strive to develop a coherent, cohesive, and fluent response. Remember that analysis is the act of breaking something down into its components to see how well they relate to each other. The components of the argument may include facts, statistics or other figures, and both stated and unstated assumptions. For example, the owner of Gemma's Jewelry store may predict that, based on the past two years' sales, the store will see an increase of 10% in next year's sales. One of the unstated assumptions is that the demand for luxury goods will increase despite whatever else may happen to the economy. Gemma's Jewelry doesn't say what will account for the increase in sales. Will the store add new lines of merchandise? Will the store increase its advertising? Will the store expand in size? Is a 10% increase significant? If sales were $40,000 last year, is an additional $4,000 dollars in sales meaningful?

You will not need knowledge in any specific discipline to analyze an argument. The topics are of general interest and are accessible to anyone regardless of previous course work. The GRE essay readers will be looking for your ability to reason and organize your thoughts in a logical way. The scoring guide that follows is reprinted from the Practice Book for the GRE Revised General Test, developed by Educational Testing Service.

Scoring Guide

Score 6

In addressing the specific task directions, a 6 response presents a cogent, well-articulated analysis of the issue and conveys meaning skillfully.

A typical response in this category:

a) articulates a clear and insightful position on the issue in accordance with the assigned task

b) develops the position fully with compelling reasons and/or persuasive examples

c) sustains a well-focused, well-organized analysis, connecting ideas logically

d) conveys ideas fluently and precisely, using effective vocabulary and sentence variety

e) demonstrates facility with the conventions of standard written English (i.e., grammar, usage and mechanics), but may have minor errors

Score 5

In addressing the specific task directions, a 5 response presents a generally thoughtful, well-developed analysis of the issue and conveys meaning clearly.

A typical response in this category:

a) presents a clear and well-considered position on the issue in accordance with the assigned task

b) develops the position with logically sound reasons and/or well-chosen examples

c) is focused and generally well organized, connecting ideas appropriately

d) conveys ideas clearly and well, using appropriate vocabulary and sentence variety

e) demonstrates facility with the conventions of standard written English but may have minor errors

Score 4

In addressing the specific task directions, a 4 response presents a competent analysis of the issue and conveys meaning with acceptable clarity.

A typical response in this category:

a) presents a clear position on the issue in accordance with the assigned task

b) develops the position with relevant reasons and/or examples

c) is adequately focused and organized

d) demonstrates sufficient control of language to express ideas with reasonable clarity

e) generally demonstrates control of the conventions of standard written English but may have some errors

Score 3

A three response demonstrates some competence in addressing the specific task directions, in analyzing the issue and in conveying meaning, but is obviously flawed.

A typical response in this category exhibits ONE OR MORE of the following characteristics:

a) is vague or limited in addressing the specific task directions and/or in presenting or developing a position on the issue

b) is weak in the use of relevant reasons or examples or relies largely on unsupported claims

c) is poorly focused and/or poorly organized

d) has problems in language and sentence structure that result in a lack of clarity

e) contains occasional major errors or frequent minor errors in grammar, usage or mechanics that can interfere with meaning

Score 2

A two response largely disregards the specific task directions and/or demonstrates serious weaknesses in analytical writing.

A typical response in this category exhibits ONE OR MORE of the following characteristics:

a) is unclear or seriously limited in addressing the specific task directions and/or in presenting or developing a position on the issue

b) provides few, if any, relevant reasons or examples in support of its claims

c) is unfocused and/or disorganized

d) has serious problems in language and sentence structure that frequently interfere with meaning

e) contains serious errors in grammar, usage or mechanics that frequently obscure meaning

Score 1

A one response demonstrates fundamental deficiencies in analytical writing.

A typical response in this category exhibits ONE OR MORE of the following characteristics:

a) provides little or no evidence of understanding the issue

b) provides little evidence of the ability to develop an organized response (i.e., is extremely disorganized and/or extremely brief)

c) has severe problems in language and sentence structure that persistently interfere with meaning

d) contains pervasive errors in grammar, usage or mechanics that result in incoherence

Score 0

A typical response in this category is off topic (i.e., provides no evidence of an attempt to respond to the assigned topic), is in a foreign language, merely copies the topic, consists of only keystroke characters or is illegible or nonverbal.

5

Solved Argument Tasks with Strategies

General Strategies

The brief passages and directions in the Analyze an Argument task contain some complexity. In order to achieve a high score, you must understand the terminology. The following list is intended to help you clarify your written evaluation of the argument.

Although you do not need to know special analytical techniques and terminology, you should be familiar with the directions for the Argument task and with certain key concepts, including the following:

a) Is there an alternative explanation for the events in question that can invalidate, either in whole or in part, the explanation given in the passage?

b) How can I break the argument into its component parts to understand how they create the whole argument?

c) Can I identify the line of reasoning used to create the argument?

d) What does the author of the argument assume to be true for the argument to be true?

e) Does the line of reasoning validate the conclusion?

f) Can I imagine an example that refutes any or several of the statements in the argument?

g) Am I able to evaluate the argument based on the quality of the facts and reasons presented in it?

Regardless of the approach you take, you must present a well-developed evaluation of the argument. You should take brief notes when you identify the arguments claims, assumptions, and conclusion. Jot down as many alternative explanations as you can along with additional evidence that might support or refute the claims in the argument. Finally, list the changes in the argument that would make the reasoning more solid. It is more important to be specific than it is to have a long list of evidence and examples.

Use as many or as few paragraphs as you consider appropriate for your argument, but you should create a new paragraph when you move on to a new idea or example of support for your position. The GRE readers are not looking for a specific number of ideas or paragraphs. Instead, they are reading to determine the level of understanding of the topic and the complexity with which you respond.

You are free to organize and develop your response in any way you think will enable you to effectively communicate your evaluation of the argument. You may recall writing strategies that you learned in high school or a writing-intensive course that you took in college, but it is not necessary to employ any of those strategies. It is important that your ideas follow a logical progression and display strong critical thinking.

Argument Task 1

Woven baskets characterized by a particular distinctive pattern have previously been found only in the immediate vicinity of the prehistoric village of Palea and therefore were believed to have been made only by the Palean people. Recently, however, archaeologists discovered such a "Palean" basket in Lithos, an ancient village across the Brim River from Palea. The Brim River is very deep and broad, and so the ancient Paleans could have crossed it only by boat, and no Palean boats have been found. Thus it follows that the so-called Palean baskets were not uniquely Palean.

Write a response in which you discuss what specific evidence is needed to evaluate the argument and explain how the evidence would weaken or strengthen the argument.

Strategies

The first step in performing your analysis consists of identifying the texts' key point, recommendation, prediction or hypothesis. All the other arguments and assumptions are designed to support this central claim. In this case, the author attempts to demonstrate that "Palean baskets were not uniquely Palean".

The next step would involve creating a statement that summarizes the text by including the central claim and its supporting arguments.

The author theorizes that the Palean baskets are no longer considered to be unique since a similar basket has been discovered in a different settlement that could only be reached by boat and the Paleans did not posses navigational means.

When considering the evidence that is necessary to support the arguments outlined in the text, it is important to keep in mind that arguments are based on assumptions – points that are taken to be true, without need for proof. This is what you need to look for – explicit and implicit assumptions, since they require evidence that is not already listed in the text. Explicit assumptions can be broken down into or supported by implicit assumptions.

Assumptions

Explicit Assumptions	Implicit assumptions
The basket found in Lithos was crafted there	Lithos or the surrounding area has the raw materials necessary to make baskets
	Lithos people have the woodworking skills required to make the baskets
	The basket that was found in Lithos is made from raw materials that can be found in the area
The Brim River was broad and deep in the prehistoric period	The prehistoric water levels of the Brim River were high
	The prehistoric water levels of the Brim River were consistently high
Prehistoric deep river crossing could only be done by boat	There were no other viable river crossing methods available at that time
	From a geographical standpoint, Lithos could only be reached by crossing the river
Only Paleans could have transported the basket across the river	Lithos is not a maritime community
	Paleans did not trade with Lithos or any maritime communities
	There are no other maritime communities in the area
Boat findings are a sufficient indicator of the presence or absence of a maritime culture	The area's climate and geological history can preserve boat remains
	There are no other sources that can indicate the existence of a maritime culture

Evidence

a) Historical or geological records indicating the presence of pliable or fibrous material in Lithos

b) Weaving tool findings in Lithos

c) The presence of artifacts crafted using similar woodworking techniques in Lithos

d) Comparison of the Lithos basket materials with the raw materials available at the time in the area

e) Geographical records of the prehistoric water levels of the Brim River (sedimentation, digital elevation etc.)

f) Prehistoric rainfall records in the area

g) River crossing methods available in the time period and area

h) Geological map of the area in prehistoric times (cave systems, the river's paleo-shorelines)

i) Boat findings in Lithos

j) Historical records of the navigational means available in Lithos (written or oral history, carvings, cave paintings etc.)

k) The presence of distinctively foreign artifacts in Palea belonging to settlements from across the river

l) The number of Palean artifacts found in settlements from across the river

m) Boat findings in the area

n) Historical records of the navigational means available in the settlements in the area (written or oral history, carvings, cave paintings etc.)

o) Comparison of the area's climate and geographical history with the conditions that are necessary for boat preservation

p) Alternative historical sources related to the navigational means available in Palea

Sample Essay

The author theorizes that the Palean baskets are no longer considered to be unique since a similar basket has been discovered in a different settlement that could only be reached by boat and the Paleans did not posses navigational means. More detailed information is necessary in order to be able to evaluate the truth of this claim.

The most compelling bit of evidence that is missing from the author's argument is related to the historical water levels of the Brim River. The writer assumes that since the Brim River is currently broad and deep the conditions must have been similar in the past. However, river levels fluctuate widely and periods of drought can severely affect the breadth and depth of a river. In order to support his claim, the author should consider the geographical records of the prehistoric water levels of the Brim River and the prehistoric rainfall records in the area. Based on this data, should the Brim River prove to have been consistently high in the time period when the Palea village existed, then it becomes less likely that the Palean style basket found in Lithos could have been carried across the river without the aid of a boat. Conversely, should the evidence show that the Brim River had low water levels in the prehistoric period, or the Palea region experienced periods of severe drought, then it becomes more likely that the Brim River could be crossed without a boat. In this case, the presence of a Palean basket in Lithos could be seen as evidence of trade rather than of Lithos developing a similar weaving style.

When making his case that the Palean basket was never transported across the river, the author assumes that deep river crossing is only possible with the aid of a boat. In order to be able to prove this claim, the author needs to look into what river crossing methods were available at the time and if there were any other geological possibilities of reaching Lithos, such as cave systems connecting the two banks of the river.

The next step in the author's argument relies on the assumption that only Paleans could have transported the basket across the river. In order to support this claim, the writer would need to show that neither Lithos nor any of the surrounding communities would have possessed the means of transporting the basket across the river. The most direct way to investigate this would involve looking at records of boat findings in Lithos or the surrounding area. Additional sources such as cave paintings, carvings or historical records depicting boats can also be used to determine whether the settlements in the area possessed a maritime culture. For instance, ancient Egypt, a civilization built on river trading, has many visual representations of boats and a history of nautical trading depicted in hieroglyphs. In the absence of boat findings or cultural evidence, trading records can also be used to demonstrate whether or not Palea had any contact with settlements from across the Brim River. Such trading evidence can come in the form of distinctively foreign artifacts in Palea belonging to settlements from across the river, or the other way around, Palean artifacts found in settlements from across the river. Should this evidence prove that it is possible that the basket found in Lithos is a result of trading, then the main claim that the Palean baskets are not uniquely Palean would be severely weakened.

When arguing that the absence of boat findings in Palea shows that Paleans could not have transported the basket across the river, the author assumes that boat findings are a sufficient indicator of the presence or absence of a maritime culture. A comparison of the area's climate and geographical history with the conditions that are necessary for boat preservation would make it easier to state with a certainty whether or not Paleans could cross the river.

Another assumption made by the author of the text is that the basket found in Lithos was crafted there. In order to assess the validity of this statement, the author should analyze whether or not the people of Lithos had the ability to produce the basket that was found there. He would first need to establish if the Lithos people had the necessary raw materials to produce the baskets. This can be accomplished by looking at historical or geological records indicating the presence of pliable or fibrous material in Lithos. This evidence would not be sufficient to either prove or disprove the claim. The author would further have to demonstrate that not just general weaving materials, but also the specific materials required for the basket can be found in the area. However, the argument would still be incomplete without the data that demonstrates that the people of Lithos had the necessary skills to make the basket. Such evidence could be gained by examining records detailing the presence of weaving tools in Lithos, or the presence of artifacts crafted using woodworking techniques similar to those required to make the basket.

All in all, additional evidence should make the author's claims harder to refute, and help prevent him from drawing faulty conclusions based on inaccurate or incomplete data.

Argument Task 2

The following appeared as a letter to the editor from a Central Plaza store owner.

"Over the past two years, the number of shoppers in Central Plaza has been steadily decreasing while the popularity of skateboarding has increased dramatically. Many Central Plaza store owners believe that the decrease in their business is due to the number of skateboard users in the plaza. There has also been a dramatic increase in the amount of litter and vandalism throughout the plaza. Thus, we recommend that the city prohibit skateboarding in Central Plaza. If skateboarding is prohibited here, we predict that business in Central Plaza will return to its previously high levels.

Write a response in which you discuss what questions would need to be answered in order to decide whether the recommendation is likely to have the predicted result. Be sure to explain how the answers to these questions would help to evaluate the recommendation.

Strategies

The first step in performing your analysis consists of identifying the texts' key point, recommendation, prediction or hypothesis. All the other arguments and assumptions are designed to support this central claim. In this case, the author attempts to demonstrate that "A skateboarding prohibition will return Central Plaza to its previously high levels".

The next step would involve creating a statement that summarizes the text by including the central claim and its supporting arguments.

The Central Plaza store owner predicts that placing a skateboarding ban in the plaza will restore its economic profitability, given that the increase in the number of skateboarders is the likeliest cause of the increase of vandalism and decrease of business in the area.

When considering what questions are needed to evaluate the arguments outlined in the text, it is important to keep in mind that arguments are based on assumptions – points that are taken to be true, without need for proof. This is what you need to look for – explicit and implicit assumptions, since they lack the evidence required to prove their validity.

Assumptions

Explicit Assumptions	Implicit Assumptions
Skateboarders are responsible for the decrease of shoppers and business	Shoppers are severely bothered by skateboarders
	Skateboarders are the main reason why shopper traffic has decreased
	Skateboarders are the main reason why business revenues have decreased
	First the skateboarders appeared and then the number of shoppers decreased
Skateboarders are the cause of littering and vandalism in the area	Vandalism and littering can be linked to the decrease in traffic and business
	Only skateboarders could have committed the vandalism and littering acts
	The vandalism can be directly linked to the skateboarders
A skateboarding ban will restore foot traffic and business revenues in the area	Skateboarders will respect the ban
	Vandalism and littering will diminish
	Customers that left because of the increase in skateboarder numbers will return to the plaza once the ban is instated
	Traffic will increase sufficiently to restore business revenues

Sample Essay

The Central Plaza store owner predicts that placing a skateboarding ban in the plaza will restore its economic profitability, given that the increase in the number of skateboarders is the likeliest cause of the increase of vandalism and decrease of business in the area. There are a number of questions that need to be taken into consideration in order to be able to evaluate how effective is the store owner's proposal.

The first thing that comes to mind when looking at the data presented in the letter is related to how much people are actually bothered by the increase in skateboarders. A possible answer to this question would be that shoppers experience only mild annoyance due to the number of skateboarders, and therefore skateboarding would not constitute the reasons for the decrease in shopper traffic. The alternative answer would entail that the people express being severely bothered by the presence of skateboarders in the plaza, to the point where they would not want to shop there anymore. In this case, the skateboarding ban would be effective in preventing more people to abandon the plaza, and with sufficient time, the traffic in the area would be restored.

When making the recommendation to ban skateboarding in Central Plaza, the store owner assumes that skateboarders are the major cause for the area's decrease in shopper traffic and business revenue. In order to be able to make this claim, the shop owner should first try to figure out if there are any other reasons for the decrease in traffic and business. Should skateboarders prove to be the sole cause for the economical downturn of the plaza, then it is possible that the area would be restored once the ban is instated. The presence of other reasons like the appearance of a new shopping center, the start of the financial crisis or better competitor prices would suggest that the ban would be ineffective in restoring the economical health of the area, and the Central Plaza storeowners should invest time and money into finding solutions for these causes, like redefining their pricing strategy or launching promotional campaigns.

The storeowner's letter also begs the question of which process came first – the increase in skateboarders or the decrease in business. The increase of skateboarders before the reduction in shopper numbers would suggest that skateboarders could be a possible cause of the declining economical health of the area, but it does not necessarily imply that they are the main cause, as seen above with the other listed potential explanations. However, should the opposite become evident, namely that the amount of shoppers coming to the plaza started declining before the skateboarders began frequenting the area, then this evidence would remove the blame from the skateboarders, since the problem existed beforehand. It is possible that skateboarders only started coming into the area because of the low foot traffic – a big open area with few numbers of people is more conductive to skateboarding than a bustling shopping center.

The storeowner's letter seems to strongly suggest that there is a link between skateboarders and the vandalism and littering in the area. Before resting the blame squarely on the shoulders of a single group of people, the store owner should ask himself whether there are any other possible vandalism culprits aside from skateboarders. The existence of other groups that are capable of committing the crime in the area means that a skateboarding ban is less likely to put a stop to the vandalism in the area. If there are no other groups in the area that could commit the crime, then the possibility that the skateboarders are responsible for the vandalism increases tenfold. In this case a skateboarding ban will have a great impact on the number of vandalism acts committed during shopping times, and depending on the customer's opinion on the deterrent effect of vandalism, it might even increase traffic in the area. This point raises another valid question that needs to be answered before the recommendations of the letter are implemented, namely : is vandalism related to the decrease in business and shopper traffic? If people consider it a major deterrent to shopping in Central Plaza then a skateboarding ban has a chance of invigorating the area's foot traffic, should skateboarders prove to be responsible for the acts. In this case a better use of resources would be to investigate and corroborate with the local police agents in order to discover the culprits, or organize patrols at night, when the crimes are most likely to occur. Should the vandalism prove to be unimportant to the people's decisions of shopping in the area it would not have much of a bearing on whether or not a skateboarding ban would be efficient.

The storeowners' assumption that skateboarders might be responsible for the vandalism in the area needs to be supported by evidence, in order to validate the claim. The store owners of Central Plaza should first investigate whether there is any evidence directly linking the vandalism to the skateboarders before making their decision. Any kind of physical evidence like camera footage, or witness testimonies would be highly helpful in assessing the claim in the letter. The existence of such evidence would also make it easier to take action by involving the police in the proceedings.

Another question that comes to mind when analyzing the effects of the skateboarding ban on the plaza's economy is whether or not the skateboarders will actually respect the ban, once it is in place. If the answer to that question is no, then even if the skateboarders were to blame for the decrease in shoppers, the implementation of the measure would be useless since it would not be effective in deterring skateboarders from coming to the plaza. Should skateboarders be inclined to respect the ban, then its overall effectiveness would still depend on people's attitudes towards skateboarding.

All the issues discussed above represent just a small amount of the questions that need to be taken into consideration by the Central Plaza store owners so that they can have a better overview of the situation before making a decision. Much more evidence than what is presented in the letter needs to be brought to attention so that the shop owners can make an informed decision.

Argument Task 3

In surveys Mason City residents rank water sports (swimming, boating, and fishing) among their favorite recreational activities. The Mason River flowing through the city is rarely used for these pursuits, however, and the city park department devotes little of its budget to maintaining riverside recreational facilities. For years there have been complaints from residents about the quality of the river's water and the river's smell. In response, the state has recently announced plans to clean up Mason River. Use of the river for water sports is, therefore, sure to increase. The city government should for that reason devote more money in this year's budget to riverside recreational facilities.

Write a response in which you examine the stated and/or unstated assumptions of the argument. Be sure to explain how the argument depends on these assumptions and what the implications are for the argument if the assumptions prove unwarranted.on.

Strategies

The first step in performing your analysis consists of identifying the texts' key point, recommendation, prediction or hypothesis. All the other arguments and assumptions are designed to support this central claim. In this case, the author attempts to argue that "The city government should devote more money to riverside recreational facilities".

The next step would involve creating a statement that summarizes the text by including the central claim and its supporting arguments.

Given the Mason City surveys ranking water sports as the favorite recreation activity of the residents and the upcoming river cleansing project that is thought to eliminate the cause for the low river usage, the author of the text argues for an increase in this year's budget devoted to riverside recreational facilities.

The easiest way to break down an argument into implicit assumptions is to look at the ideas that support each core (explicit) assumption. Ideally, it would be good to have at least three implicit assumption for every explicit one. However, keep in mind that you likely won't have time enough to expound on all of them in your essay. When writing your argument it's good to lay down the ideas like in the format below – it will help you more easily determine which explicit assumptions are undermined/strengthened by the implicit argument you are analyzing.

Assumptions

Explicit Assumptions	Implicit Assumptions
Survey accurately reflects people's opinions on water sports	There are no biased or leading questions
	The survey demographics are representative of the city (city and survey demographics are similar)
	The studies have a low standard deviation (enough people participated, so that a small group's opinion cannot skew the results)
	People that rank water sports as high will also participate in them
River pollution is responsible for the low usage of the city river	The complaints are representative for the city
	River pollution is the only reason why people do not use the river
Cleaning up the river will increase usage for water sports	There are no other outlets for water sports in the city
	The smell of the river is due to pollution and not a naturally occurring event (sulphur)
	The quality of the water is due to pollution and not a natural occurring event (mineral deposits)
	Residents would like to use the river for water sports
	The clean-up will end pollution/is extensive
The increase in usage is sufficient to justify increasing the budget for riverside recreational facilities	A great percentage of people will go to the riverside
	The people that go to the riverside need facilities
	Riverside facilities are dedicated to water sports (and not other pursuits)
	Current riverside facilities are insufficient
	The clean-up of the river will happen in a short term (enough to justify making changes to this years budget)

After having established your assumptions you need to take care of the second part of your essay, namely the implications for the main claim should the assumptions be unwarranted. A good way to go about writing this part is to think of examples of situations that may contradict each implicit assumption. The examples are not vital, you can still build a case by directly stating " if assumption 'A' proves to be untrue, then…" . However, including the contradicting situations will help enrich your essay and ultimately get you a higher score.

The next step would be to create a 'logic tree' to see how disproving an assumption will affect the other arguments down the line. The branch of the logic tree will follow this line: implicit assumption affects explicit assumptions which in turn relate to the main argument.

For instance, in our case:

Implicit assumption	Contradicting situations	Effect on explicit assumption	Effect on main argument
River pollution is the only reason why people do not use the river	- river is too distant - very fast currents	-somewhat weaken or disprove the assumption (people might still not use the river after it is cleaned)	- building more facilities would become useless, if river usage will not increase - waste of resources
The smell of the river is due to pollution and not a naturally occurring event	- sulfur - natural gas leaks (Cattaraugus Creek)	- cleaning the river will not remove the odor - cleaning the river will not increase river usage	- building more facilities would become useless, if river usage will not increase - waste of resources
The complaints are representative for the city	- low percentage of people complaining - an individual filing a large number of complaints	- the complaints do not reflect the resident's opinions about the river - river usage might not increase by solving the complaints	- building more facilities would become useless, if river usage will not increase - main cause of low river usage remains unknown

Sample Essay

Given the Mason City surveys ranking water sports as the favorite recreation activity of the residents and the upcoming river cleansing project that is thought to eliminate the cause for the low river usage, the author of the text argues for an increase in this year's budget devoted to riverside recreational facilities. The author of the proposal makes suggestions that can prove to be very costly especially if the assumptions on which the case rests prove to be unwarranted.

When arguing for the increased revenue allocated to this year's budget for riverside facilities, the author draws upon data from surveys conducted in Mason City. One of the main assumptions that the case rests on is that the surveys that were conducted accurately reflect people's opinions on water sports. In taking this data at face value, the author further assumes that the survey demographics are representative for the entirety of the city. The most essential part of any research is the methodology – in this case, if the survey takers asked only people that live next to the river or only citizens of a certain age, then that can very well mean that the rest of the citizens do not view water sports as a favorite activity, in which case, regardless of the river cleaning actions, the actual usage of the waterway will not increase.

Another implicit assumption related to the idea that the surveys accurately reflect people's opinions on water sports is the notion that the research methodology is sound, namely there are no biased or leading questions. Phrasing survey questions is sometimes likened to an art – just like any activity that requires a considerable amount of skill and knowledge. Should the surveys contain badly phrased questions, like an option to chose between water sports or extreme activities, then the results of the surveys would no longer be reliable. In this example, most people would choose water sports because it is the less extreme/unreasonable option and not because they would like to actively engage in this type of sporting activity. In this case, a budgetary increase for riverside facilities could prove to be a waste of money, since people's interests lie elsewhere, and not with river based activities. The same conclusion would apply if the questions were biased due to the personal interest of the survey researchers (a company providing water sports equipment can be unwittingly biased and skewer the results in favor of water sports activities simply by placing the focus of the questionnaire on said type of activity).

Another line of reasoning that the author uses to support his argument is the idea that river pollution and odor are responsible for the low usage of the city river. This argument is based on several other assumptions like the notion that the complaints received about river odor and pollution are representative for the city and the idea that there are no other possible explanations as to why the river usage is low. It is entirely within the realm of possibility that the overall number of complaints, when reported to the total number of citizens, is very low. Or, if the number of complaints is high, it may well be that only a small number of people are responsible for them (in the sense that a single person files a large number of complaints). In both of these instances, the complaints prove not to be representative for the overall opinion of the citizens. If that is the case, and this assumption is unwarranted, then the upcoming cleaning of the river will not address the main cause of the low river usage and the number of people engaging in sporting activities on the waterway will remain unaffected. As such, increasing the budget for riverside facilities would be pointless, not to mention costly.

The other assumption supporting the idea that the river pollution and odor are responsible for the low usage of the city river is the notion that there are no other possible explanations as to why the river usage is low. If there are other reasons why people don't like to use the Mason City river, like the distance to the river or the presence of strong currents, then the cleaning of the river would fail to address the people's main concerns with the waterway, and river usage will not increase.

These lines of inquiry lead directly to another main assumption on which the author rests his case for increasing the amount of money allocated to riverside facilities. The author assumes that cleaning up the river will increase the river's usage for water sports. When advocating for this line of thought, the author assumes that the smell and quality of the water are due to pollution, and not naturally occurring events. Sulfur in the water can give it a rotten egg smell, or the presence of natural gas in the river banks can create a foul odor. As for the water quality, mineral deposits in the water or an abundance of underwater plant life can give the river an unappealing look. These are just some of the possible alternate explanation for the river's odor and water quality. If there are natural causes for the look and odor of the river, then cleaning the river will not get rid of either problem. Provided that most citizens consider the river's look and odor to be the main deterrent against doing sporting activities on the Mason City river, then river usage would not increase with the cleansing of the river. As such, the proposal to increase funds for riverside facilities would not be supported by a rise in actual usage of those facilities.

When proposing to increase the money allocated to the riverside facilities in Mason City, the author of the argument assumes that there will be a sufficient increase in river usage to justify taking these budgetary measures. An implicit assumption of this argument is the idea that a great percentage of people will go to the riverside. If, for instance, there are a lot of water sport outlets in town, due to the river being unappealing and the resident of Mason City loving water based activities, then it's entirely likely that even after the river is made accessible, a great percentage of the population will continue to use those outlets (especially since they like to offer subscriptions). Should that be the case, and the number of people that would go to the riverside would be low, then there would be no justification to increase the budget for riverside facilities.

All in all, when making the case for increasing the budget for the riverside facilities in Mason City, the author of the proposal makes a series of assumptions that are not backed by evidence and would require further investigation. Spending taxpayer money always needs good justification – without a more thorough investigation, the author risks of drawing inaccurate conclusions which will lead to making ineffective or costly suggestions.

Argument Task 4

Two years ago, radio station WCQP in Rockville decided to increase the number of call-in advice programs that it broadcast; since that time, its share of the radio audience in the Rockville listening area has increased significantly. Given WCQP's recent success with call-in advice programming, and citing a nationwide survey indicating that many radio listeners are quite interested in such programs, the station manager of KICK in Medway recommends that KICK include more call-in advice programs in an attempt to gain a larger audience share in its listening area.

Write a response in which you discuss what questions would need to be answered in order to decide whether the recommendation is likely to have the predicted result. Be sure to explain how the answers to these questions would help to evaluate the recommendation.

Strategies

The first step in performing your analysis consists of identifying the texts' key point, recommendation, prediction or hypothesis. All the other arguments and assumptions are designed to support this central claim. In this case, the author attempts to demonstrate that "more call in advice program will increase the stations' listener ratings".

The next step would involve creating a statement that summarizes the text by including the central claim and its supporting arguments.

The station manager of KICK recommends increasing the number of call-in advice programs that are being broadcasted in order to gain a larger audience, given that a similar strategy has worked for a radio station in another town, and a national survey indicates that people are interested in such programs.

When considering what questions are needed to evaluate the arguments outlined in the text, it is important to keep in mind that arguments are based on assumptions – points that are taken to be true, without need for proof. This is what you need to look for – explicit and implicit assumptions, since they lack the evidence required to prove their validity.

Assumptions

Explicit Assumptions	Implicit Assumptions
WCQP's increase in listeners is due to the additional call-in advice programs	There were no other internal factors that could have contributed to WCQP's increase in listener ratings
	There were no other external (economical) factors that could have contributed to the increase in listener ratings
	The increase in listener ratings is for the call-in advice time slot
	The increase in listeners was significant
The national survey accurately reflects the preferences of Medway's population	Demographics of both Medway and the survey are compatible
	The survey findings are conclusive
The strategy applied in Rockville is applicable in Medway	Rockville and Medway have similar target audience demographics
	WCQP and KICK have similar market situations
	WCQP and KICK are comparable in terms of size and popularity
KICK's audience will increase with more call-in advice programs	Medway's radio listener market size is big enough to support the potential audience growth
	There is a need for call-in advice programs
	The need for call-in advice programs was not met elsewhere

Sample Essay

The station manager of KICK recommends increasing the number of call-in advice programs that are being broadcasted in order to gain a larger audience, given that a similar strategy has worked for a radio station in another town, and a national survey indicates that people are interested in such programs. Like all changes to a business' approach, the recommendation made by KICK's manager carries with it a risk of failure, and as such needs to be thoroughly analyzed before any decisions of implementing the suggested strategy are made.

In outlining his reasoning for the recommendation, the station manager of KICK rests his case on the assumption that WCQP's increase in listeners is due to the additional call-in advice programs. The first question that comes into mind, in this case, is if there were any other internal and external factors that could have contributed to the increase in listeners, such as a shutdown of one of WCQP's major competitors, the start of a WCQP promotional campaign or the station acquiring a popular radio host. Having a great number of other plausible explanations for WCQP's success would significantly weaken the premise that more call-in advice programs would have the desired effect on KICK's listener basis. However, should the answer to the question prove that the increase in call-in advice programs is the sole or major reason responsible for the listener audience boost, then it becomes plausible that WCQP's success can be replicated by KICK, given additional compatibility points like market analysis data.

The next inquiry point related to WCQP's success would investigate during which time slot did the WCQP listener ratings increase and how significant was this increase. This data can serve to research whether the listener increase is statistically relevant. A rise in listener ratings of 1%, while technically still considered an increase, would mean that adding more call-in advice programs is a costly method with no substantial benefits and the station managers should consider alternate means of bolstering listener ratings. From the other perspective, should it turn out that the increase in audience market shares is a dramatic one, then KICK's managers should give the WCQP's strategy due consideration.

When making his case for increasing the amount of call-in advice programs the station manager cites the results of a national survey as compelling evidence that there is a great desire for programs of this type. When handling surveys and statistic data it is always important to look not only at the results but also at the theoretical framework and methodology of the study being conducted, in order to be able to ascertain whether the reasoning is sound, or if the scientists have missed some crucial aspect or mitigating factor. As such, the station manager should inquire as to how accurate are the study findings. Should the methodology be faulty, like having a small sample size with a big standard deviation, or constructing the survey questions in a leading manner, then the results would no longer be indicative of the people's desire for listening to call-in programs, and the station manager would have to find alternative means of estimating the potential market size, lest his argument becomes significantly weakened. A properly conducted survey can serve to strengthen the station manager's recommendation – most market analyses are based on such type of direct information gathering.

If the survey findings are accurate, then the next step would be to determine whether these results are applicable to the population of Medway. The station manager should ask himself if the survey and Medway's demographics are compatible. If this assumption holds true, then the manager has accurately pinpointed a current need of the Medway population and the recommendation to satisfy said need by changing their programs would be more warranted. But national studies deal with averages, therefore it is possible that what might be true for the general population is not necessarily true for a particular subgroup. For instance a national study that identified the preferred musical genres as rock and oldies might not be so applicable to specific cases, like towns from the bible belt. Should the demographics not be comparable, then the national survey that is at the center of the station manager's argument would not accurately reflect the preferences of the local population of Medway. In order to strengthen his argument, the station manager would have to look at radio preference indicators that are specific to Medway.

The station manager's assumption that the strategy applied in Rockville is applicable in Medway begets the question of how similar the Medway and Rockville markets and target audiences are to each other. If the target audience demographics and the market conditions like the number of competitors, market size or degree of popularity are relatively similar, then implementing the suggested strategy would be a very good course of action, given the high likelihood of replicating WCQP's success. Not only that, but the similarity can make the strategy very cost effective and provide KICK with a readymade implementation roadmap that has a high probability of increasing the company's profits. However, if the market and target audiences of the two cities are different, then the assumption that the strategy applied in Rockville is applicable in Medway is significantly weakened, because there is a high likelihood that WCQP's success strategy might not be suitable for the population of Medway. In order to deal with this possibility, the station manager would have to adapt the finer points of WCQP's strategy to the needs of the Medway population, in which case his recommendation might still be valid. Current trendsetting strategies also rely heavily on the reuse of successful strategies with adaptations made to suit each company's specific situation.

All in all, before arguing for the implementation of a strategy used by a different radio station, KICK's station manager should consider whether the market conditions in the two towns are similar enough to warrant making the suggested change. The manager should also consider how to adapt the strategies if the markets prove to be too different, or completely reorient himself to other strategies, based on market demands.

Argument Task 5

The following is a memorandum from the business manager of a television station.

"Over the past year, our late-night news program has devoted increased time to national news and less time to weather and local news. During this time period, most of the complaints received from viewers were concerned with our station's coverage of weather and local news. In addition, local businesses that used to advertise during our late-night news program have just canceled their advertising contracts with us. Therefore, in order to attract more viewers to the program and to avoid losing any further advertising revenues, we should restore the time devoted to weather and local news to its former level."

Write a response in which you discuss what specific evidence is needed to evaluate the argument and explain how the evidence would weaken or strengthen the argument

NOTE: The above topic has wording similar to Agrument Task 13 of GRE Analytical Writing Solutions to the Real Essay Topics - Book 1. However, if you read carefully you will notice that the task instructions are different. Hence, it is very important to read the topic as well as its instructions completely before you start to write your response.

Strategies

The first step in performing your analysis consists of creating a statement that summarizes the text by including the central claim and its supporting arguments.

The business manager of a television station is arguing for reverting to the predominantly local weather and news coverage in a bid to increase viewer ratings and prevent further loss of funds from advertising cancelations.

When considering the evidence that is necessary to support the arguments outlined in the text, it is important to keep in mind that arguments are based on assumptions – points that are taken to be true, without need for proof. This is what you need to look for – explicit and implicit assumptions, since they require evidence that is not already listed in the text. Explicit assumptions can be broken down into or supported by implicit assumptions.

Assumptions

<table>
<tr><th>Explicit Assumptions</th><th>Implicit Assumptions</th></tr>
<tr><td rowspan="4">Complaints about national weather and news coverage indicate a desire for more local programs</td><td>The complaints are related to the national character of the weather and news coverage</td></tr>
<tr><td>Local coverage receiver less or no complaints</td></tr>
<tr><td>Complaints are linked to viewer ratings</td></tr>
<tr><td>The complaints are representative for the entire audience of the late night news program</td></tr>
<tr><td rowspan="3">Advertising cancelations are due to the increase in time devoted to national news</td><td>Add cancelation is not due to external circumstances</td></tr>
<tr><td>The rate of cancellations has increased</td></tr>
<tr><td>Local as opposed to national coverage has an impact on the local companies' business</td></tr>
<tr><td rowspan="3">Viewer ratings will increase by reverting to a predominantly local news coverage</td><td>Local coverage had higher viewer ratings than national coverage</td></tr>
<tr><td>The viewer's desires for local coverage are not met elsewhere</td></tr>
<tr><td>Late night news market has the potential for growth</td></tr>
<tr><td rowspan="3">Reverting to local news will prevent other businesses from cancelling their advertising contracts</td><td>Local businesses would welcome the change</td></tr>
<tr><td>Businesses that have current ad contracts would not have other reasons for cancelling</td></tr>
<tr><td>The area will continue to be economically stable</td></tr>
</table>

Evidence

a) Precise nature of the complaints

b) Comparison of the number of complaints received during local and national coverage

c) Number of complaints throughout the years reported to the total number of late night news viewers

d) Comparison of the number of complaints received per type of program throughout the years

e) Comparison of ad viewer ratings during national and local coverage

f) Comparison of economical health of the region during local and national coverage

g) Compare advertisement investment numbers for local businesses during the local and national coverage

h) Compare advertisement cancellation rates during national and local coverage

i) Compare viewer rates for local and national coverage

j) Correlate the number of competitor programs offering local weather and news coverage with the size of the potential market

k) Global viewer ratings for late night news programs in the area

l) Profit and loss analysis of the local businesses currently under contract

m) Survey or interviews with the local business owners currently under contract on how they perceive the change to more local coverage

Sample Essay

The business manager of a television station is arguing for reverting to the predominantly local weather and news coverage in a bid to increase viewer ratings and prevent further loss of funds from advertising cancelations. Before implementing the manager's suggestions, the television station's board of directors needs to consider additional information. Undertaking such a change without careful consideration can run the risk of adopting costly yet ultimately unnecessary measures.

The manager's suggestions are based on the assumption that advertising cancelations are due to the increase in time devoted to national news, and reverting to local news will prevent other businesses from cancelling their current contracts. A key bit of information needed to asses this claim is related to previous cancelation rates. The manager should compare advertisement cancellation rates during both national and local coverage. This evidence would help in establishing if the cancellations are a new phenomenon, in which case, it is possible that the national character of the news is responsible, or, if cancellations are a regularly occurring phenomenon, as such, changing the nature of the late night news coverage would have little to no effect. The manager should also analyze whether there were any other external factors that could have been responsible for the local businesses' decision to terminate their advertising contracts. A comparison of the economical health of the region during local and national coverage would help illustrate whether there are any other causes for the advertisement cancellations. Should that be the case, switching to a predominantly local coverage would not have the desired effect of preventing other businesses from cancelling their contracts .

Another key bit of evidence to consider when analyzing the assumption that reverting to local news will prevent other businesses from cancelling their current contracts is a comparison of ad viewer ratings during local and national coverage. This evidence would help establish if the national or local character of the coverage has an impact on the local companies' business.

The second part of the manager's argument focuses on the audience and is based on the assumption that viewer ratings will increase by reverting to a predominantly local news coverage. In order to support this claim, the manager cites that the majority of the complaints received by the television station are related to the coverage of local weather and news. Before considering the validity of this claim, the board of directors should first look at the nature of the submitted complaints. Based on this data, should the nature of the complaints be directly related to the fact that the late night news program has a national instead of a local coverage, then the business manager's suggestion of reverting to the old model has increased merit. However, if the complaints received about the national coverage are more related to the anchormen or format of the show than the fact that it presents national and not local information, then switching to predominantly local coverage will not necessarily bring an increase in viewership.

When arguing that complaints about national weather and news coverage indicate a desire for more local programs, the television station's business manager assumes that the complaints received are representative for the entire audience of the late night news program. In order to support that claim, the author should look into what percentage from the total number of late night news viewers is represented by people who complained about the national coverage.

The business manager centers his recommendation for reverting to a predominantly local coverage on the idea that viewer ratings will increase and businesses will no longer cancel their advertising contracts.

By comparing the viewer rates for local and national coverage the author can establish if the viewers prefer local weather and news coverage to the national alternative. If that is indeed the case, barring external factors that could have influenced the results, then the evidence would serve to corroborate the manager's theory that viewer rates will be restored once the station adopts the proposed change. However, if the opposite proves to be true and viewer ratings are higher during national rather than local coverage, then the manager's proposal runs the high risk of driving audiences away rather than increasing their ratings. There is also the possibility that even if the population prefers local news, the market is saturated. In order to assess market readiness and availability, the television station's manager should correlate the number of competitor programs offering local weather and news coverage with the size of the potential market. Having the majority of the market cornered by competing local coverage programs would make the goal of increasing ratings significantly harder to reach. However, should the market be mostly free then the manager's suggestion would have a great chance of being even more successful than expected.

All in all, when making such a potentially costly decision it is essential to thoroughly investigate the benefits and devise strategies that limit the risks. The television station manager needs to provide an accurate assessment of the market situation and conduct in depth research on the target audience, lest he run the risk of making a decision that would bring loss to the station.

Argument Task 6

The following appeared in a memorandum from the owner of Movies Galore, a chain of movie-rental stores.

"In order to reverse the recent decline in our profits, we must reduce operating expenses at Movies Galore's ten movie-rental stores. Since we are famous for our special bargains, raising our rental prices is not a viable way to improve profits. Last month our store in downtown Marston significantly decreased its operating expenses by closing at 6:00 p.m. rather than 9:00 p.m. and by reducing its stock by eliminating all movies released more than five years ago. Therefore, in order to increase profits without jeopardizing our reputation for offering great movies at low prices, we recommend implementing similar changes in our other nine Movies Galore stores."

Write a response in which you discuss what questions would need to be answered in order to decide whether the recommendation and the argument on which it is based are reasonable. Be sure to explain how the answers to these questions would help to evaluate the recommendation.

Strategies

A good place to start your analysis is by creating a statement that reveals the main idea of the argument. Although the writer is creating an argument, he may ultimately be stating a position, making a recommendation, or making a prediction. It may be helpful for you to determine which of these formats is most evident in the argument.

The owner of Movies Galore is recommending the same changes in all of his stores that he made in his downtown Marston location as a means of reversing a decline in profits.

Assumptions:

a) Reducing expenses is the best way for Movies Galore to increase profits.

b) The changes made at the downtown Marston location will be successful at the other stores.

c) Low prices are the major reason people patronize Movies Galore.

d) Movies older than five years attract fewer customers than other genres or newer releases.

e) The downtown Marston location is busiest between opening and 6:00 pm.

f) The downtown Marston location is not busy enough between 6:00 and 9:00 pm to justify staying open during those hours.

Questions:

a) Have profits declined at all or just some of the stores?

b) Have profits increased at the downtown Marston store?

c) During which hours is each store busiest?

d) Has the owner tried other means of reducing expenses?

e) Why do customers choose Movies Galore?

f) Are older videos in high demand at any of the locations?

g) Has the owner made some recent changes that have had a negative impact on profits?

After completing these steps, you should have enough material to write your analysis. Remember that you are not creating a position of your own; you are evaluating the strengths and weaknesses of the existing argument. You do not have to include all of the points that you have created in your prewriting. In fact, during the process of drafting your analysis, other ideas may come to mind, and, if they strengthen your analysis, you should include them.

Sample Essay

The owner of Movies Galore has made a sweeping recommendation with a view to increasing profits for his business. Before adopting the recommendation at all of his locations, he or she needs to answer some pointed questions. One size may not fit all. Each location should be analyzed individually by examining the answers to the questions.

First, he should ask if each store is experiencing a decline in profitability. He may find that only one or two of the stores are creating the decline in profits. Those which are making money for the company should likely be left alone. Even though all of them may be losing money, each may need an individual, specific adjustment to reverse the trend. This owner should also ask what the successful stores may be doing that the others are not. The answer may lead him to make changes different from the ones in the argument.

Shortening the hours of operation and eliminating some inventory will certainly reduce expenses, but the tactic doesn't always contribute to greater profits. Has the downtown Marston store generated higher profits since the changes were made? If that store was not habitually busy between the hours of 6:00 and 9:00, then the relatively minor loss of revenue may be offset by a fairly significant decrease in operating expenses. Electricity, heat, and wages for three hours can be substantial and are aspects of a business operation that can be controlled. Was there very little demand for older videos in that location as well? If so, then money spent on inventory can be better used to stock videos in greater demand by customers in this particular store.

Assuming that the owner has made the correct business decisions for the downtown location, it might be logical to apply the same changes to the other Movies Galore stores. Do all of the other locations experience a lack of business after 6:00? Any stores located in or near a mall may be busiest during the evening hours. Malls are generally open until 9:00 at night, and a store that closes at 6:00 will not be able to take advantage of traffic generated by the other shops.

The owner of Movies Galore assumes that the low prices account for the stores' popularity, but is that really the reason that customers choose them? Movies Galore may have the best selection of the videos most in demand. The stores' locations may be convenient and have plenty of free parking. They may have a great selection of movie snacks. The staff may be friendly and helpful. Without surveying his customers, the owner could be holding onto an idea that has little to support it.

Has the owner attempted any other changes to improve profits? He could increase revenues by expanding the selection of movie snacks and training his associates to suggest patrons buy them with every rental. Customers may have abandoned Movies Galore because the videos are not organized logically or the associates deliver poor service.

Has the owner made some recent changes that have led to a temporary decline in profits? Upgrading heating systems or lighting fixtures, for example, can be costly one-time expenditures that can account for the current lack of profitability. The owner may have new employees or managers that are undercharging for rentals or who may be stealing from the company.

Are other, similar businesses in the area experiencing a similar decline in profits? If so, Movies Galore's owner may have to look at his problem in an entirely different light. The market may be over saturated with movie rental businesses. People's rental habits may have changed in recent years by using video-on-demand features through their television cable companies or by subscribing to services like Netflix. When he examines the answers to all of the questions, the owner of Movies Galore will make better-informed decisions about his business.

Argument Task 7

> *The following appeared in a memo from the vice president of a food distribution company with food storage warehouses in several cities.*
>
> *"Recently, we signed a contract with the Fly-Away Pest Control Company to provide pest control services at our warehouse in Palm City, but last month we discovered that over $20,000 worth of food there had been destroyed by pest damage. Meanwhile, the Buzzoff Pest Control Company, which we have used for many years in Palm City, continued to service our warehouse in Wintervale, and last month only $10,000 worth of the food stored there had been destroyed by pest damage. Even though the price charged by Fly-Away is considerably lower, our best means of saving money is to return to Buzzoff for all our pest control services."*
>
> *Write a response in which you discuss what questions would need to be answered in order to decide whether the recommendation and the argument on which it is based are reasonable. Be sure to explain how the answers to these questions would help to evaluate the recommendation.*

Strategies

A good place to start your analysis is by creating a statement that reveals the main idea of the argument. Although the writer is creating an argument, he may ultimately be stating a position, making a recommendation, or making a prediction. It may be helpful for you to determine which of these formats is most evident in the argument.

As a result of pest damage in the Palm City warehouse, the vice president of the food distribution company recommends a return to Buzzoff Pest Control for pest control in Palm City.

Assumptions:

a) Buzzoff Pest Control is more effective than Fly-Away.

b) Conditions at both warehouses are identical.

c) Both warehouses contain the same product.

d) A larger percentage of product was lost in Palm City than in Wintervale.

e) The amount of loss this month was greater than in previous months.

Questions:

a) Why did the food distribution company change pest-control companies at its Palm City location?

b) What types of food does the company store at each facility?

c) What percentage of the total value of food stores at each facility was destroyed by pests?

d) Is the $20,000 loss in the Palm City facility higher than normal?

e) How much product is generally lost to pest each year at each location?

f) What conditions exist at the remainder of the company's several locations?

After completing these steps, you should have enough material to write your analysis. Remember that you are not creating a position of your own; you are evaluating the strengths and weaknesses of the existing argument. You do not have to include all of the points that you have created in your prewriting. In fact, during the process of drafting your analysis, other ideas may come to mind, and, if they strengthen your analysis, you should include them.

Sample Essay

It appears that the vice president of the food distribution company has had a change of heart concerning his choice of pest control at the Palm City warehouse. The facts that he presents, on the surface, appear reasonable. Upon closer examination of the information in the recommendation, the reader may identify several questions that need answers before agreeing with the vice president.

The vice president should ask himself why he changed companies in the first place. Without more detailed information, one might assume that this vice president was dissatisfied with the service provided by Buzzoff in the Palm City location. Other, similar businesses may have recommended Fly Away as an alternative, and this vice president, seeing the reduction in price, may have accepted the recommendation without carefully examining Fly Away's record of performance. The storage company has several other locations in addition to those in Palm City and Wintervale. Which pest control companies provide services for those warehouses? How successful are they at preventing losses? If Buzzoff successfully prevents pest damage in these other locations, the company would be advised to rehire them in Palm City. It may be that the warehouse company uses one or more other companies altogether. Answers to these questions may provide evidence that the vice president's recommendation is correct, or they may show that another company altogether would be a better candidate for pest control at Palm City.

How does last month's $20,000 loss compare to losses from prior months or the same month in previous years at the Palm City location? If it is significantly higher than the average of losses in the past, the warehouse company may be justified in making the recommendation to return to Buzzoff's service. If the figure represents an average loss for that month, however, the $20,000 figure becomes irrelevant to the argument and recommendation. The same scrutiny should be applied to the Wintervale loss of product. Is a $10,000 loss typical, lower than average, or higher than average? In order for the comparison between the two locations to be valid, these questions must be answered. Is the $20,000 loss significant at all? If the company stores 2 million dollars worth of food in Palm City, the loss is only 1%. How much product is stored at each of the two facilities? If both warehouses have product with the same dollar value, then Palm City has lost twice as much as Wintervale to pest damage during the same period of time, a fact that would lead to further scrutiny of both pest control companies' practices. If Wintervale stores considerably less product than Palm City, the $10,000 loss may represent a greater portion of the total lost to pest damage and raises the question of Buzzoff's ability to provide sufficient protection against pests.

Could some other event explain the loss at Palm City? The pest damage may have occurred prior to the product's arrival at the warehouse. Containers may have been improperly closed, or refrigeration functioned defectively. If so, Fly Away cannot be held responsible for the resulting pest damage, and should not be replaced. Workers at the warehouse itself may have mishandled the product, again relieving Fly Away of responsibility for the loss of product. The county in which Wintervale is located may have initiated an aerial spraying program that made it easier, perhaps even unnecessary, for Buzzoff to control pests and incur less damage. Conversely, the county that Palm city calls home may have suspended an aerial spraying program making it more difficult to control pests in that location.

The food distribution company owns several warehouses in a variety of locations, and pest control is important for profitability. The answers to the questions will help the owner make a considered decision about the most effective means of eliminating loss in Palm City. It may turn out that they should retain Fly Away, rehire Buzzoff or use another company entirely.

Argument Task 8

Evidence suggests that academic honor codes, which call for students to agree not to cheat in their academic endeavors and to notify a faculty member if they suspect that others have cheated, are far more successful than are other methods at deterring cheating among students at colleges and universities. Several years ago, Groveton College adopted such a code and discontinued its old-fashioned system in which teachers closely monitored students. Under the old system, teachers reported an average of thirty cases of cheating per year. In the first year the honor code was in place, students reported twenty-one cases of cheating; five years later, this figure had dropped to fourteen. Moreover, in a recent survey, a majority of Groveton students said that they would be less likely to cheat with an honor code in place than without.

Write a response in which you discuss one or more alternative explanations that could rival the proposed explanation and explain how your explanation(s) can plausibly account for the facts presented in the argument.

NOTE: The above topic has wording similar to Agrument Task 15 of GRE Analytical Writing Solutions to the Real Essay Topics Book 1. However, if you read carefully you will notice that the task instructions are different. Hence, it is very important to read the topic as well as its instructions completely before you start to write your response.

Strategies

A good place to start your analysis is by creating a statement that reveals the main idea of the argument. Although the writer is creating an argument, he may ultimately be stating a position, making a recommendation, or making a prediction. It may be helpful for you to determine which of these formats is most evident in the argument.

The argument states the position that an honor code is a more effective means of curtailing cheating than close supervision by professors, and evidence at Groveton College appears to support the author's explanation.

Assumptions:

a) Instances of cheating have declined since instituting an honor code.

b) Between years one and five under the honor code system, instances of cheating continually declined.

c) Enrollment at the college has remained the same during the five years of the honor code.

d) Students are as likely to report cheating as are professors.

Alternative explanations:

a) Students are less likely to report on their peers, thereby reducing the number of recorded cases of cheating.

b) The college increased the severity of consequences for cheating when adopting the honor code.

c) Students may not recognize some forms of cheating.

d) Students don't have the opportunity to observe cheating.

e) The school may have changed its grading system.

f) Instructors may have adjusted their curriculum and assessments.

After completing these steps, you should have enough material to write your analysis. Remember that you are not creating a position of your own; you are evaluating the strengths and weaknesses of the existing argument. You do not have to include all of the points that you have created in your prewriting. In fact, during the process of drafting your analysis, other ideas may come to mind, and, if they strengthen your analysis, you should include them.

Sample Essay

The argument promotes the effectiveness of using an honor code to prevent cheating and uses some scant evidence to justify its continued use. An apparent decline in the number of cheating incidents leads the reader to agree with the position, but other explanations may be more realistic.

Students are not as likely to observe, recognize, or report cheating as are their professors. In a testing situation, for example, students may be so focused on their own performance and completing the test on time that they are unaware of others around them. Given the opportunity to look at other students in the classroom, they might not recognize that a fellow test- taker is cheating. Many who cheat have developed techniques that make their dishonest behavior invisible to the casual or inexperienced observer. Students who do see and recognize another's cheating are faced with a moral dilemma. On one hand, they have agreed to honor the code established by the college. On the other hand, they may risk losing a friend or causing the failure of an otherwise honest student. They may empathize with a classmate who chooses cheating as a means of passing a difficult course. Of course, cheating on a test is not the only form of academic dishonesty. Plagiarism rears its ugly head when students are under some pressure to meet a deadline for a research paper. The temptation to cut-and-paste and take credit for another's words or ideas is strong for college students who have run out of ideas before running out of time. Other students are not likely to see this type of work done by classmates and, therefore, cannot be expected to report it. The professors who do read and recognize the plagiarized writing are no longer compelled to report it. They may simply assign a grade of zero. These limitations can help to explain the lower number of reported incidents of cheating at Groveton College.

The adoption of the honor code by itself may not fully explain the apparent decline in cheating. School officials may have added new consequences or strengthened those that already existed if students are caught cheating in some manner. Fear of failure or expulsion would have created a greater incentive to remain academically honest at Groveton College.

In addition to instituting an honor code, Groveton College may have changed its grading system. They may have replaced a traditional 4-point measurement of excellence to pass/fail, for example. Relieved of the pressure to achieve based on rigid guidelines, students would feel less compelled to cheat in order to meet grading expectations. In addition, professors may have changed the nature of their assessments. Instead of administering tests in a pressurized classroom under time constraints, they may have given take-home tests that students can complete in the comfort of their own residences, using notes and other resources. They may have eliminated tests altogether, relying on measurements of knowledge that are less likely to create opportunities for cheating.

Perhaps the simplest explanation for a reduction in the number of reported instances of cheating would be a decline in student population at Groveton College. In fact, the college may have instituted the apparently popular honor code in an effort to attract more students to its campus. Depending on the size of the student body, a reduction in the number of reported cases of cheating could be an increase in the percentage of students caught cheating.

Groveton's use of the survey results in which a majority of students said they would be less likely to cheat if an honor code exists may be short-sighted. The survey may not have included other incentives to curtail cheating. If the survey listed only an honor code as a choice, the conclusion is flawed and is not likely to explain the apparent reduction in reported cheating cases.

If any of these alternate explanations sufficiently account for the lower number of reported cases of cheating at Groveton College, the school must relinquish its belief that the honor code is an effective change in its academic philosophy. Further investigation by college administrators can uncover the real reason for an increase in academic integrity.

Argument Task 9

The following is a recommendation from the personnel director to the president of Acme Publishing Company.

"Many other companies have recently stated that having their employees take the Easy Read Speed-Reading Course has greatly improved productivity. One graduate of the course was able to read a 500-page report in only two hours; another graduate rose from an assistant manager to vice president of the company in under a year. Obviously, the faster you can read, the more information you can absorb in a single workday. Moreover, Easy Read would cost Acme only $500 per employee - a small price to pay when you consider the benefits. Included in this fee is a three-week seminar in Spruce City and a lifelong subscription to the Easy Read newsletter. Clearly, Acme would benefit greatly by requiring all of our employees to take the Easy Read course."

Write a response in which you discuss what specific evidence is needed to evaluate the argument and explain how the evidence would weaken or strengthen the argument.

Strategies

A good place to start your analysis is by creating a statement that reveals the main idea of the argument. Although the writer is creating an argument, he may ultimately be stating a position, making a recommendation, or making a prediction. It may be helpful for you to determine which of these formats is most evident in the argument.

Based on examples from other companies, the personnel director at Acme Publishing Company is recommending the Easy Read Speed-Reading course as a means of benefiting Acme Publishing Company.

Assumptions:

a) Easy Read Speed-Reading Course increases productivity in the workplace.

b) Graduates of the course are more likely to be promoted.

c) People who read faster absorb more information.

d) Benefits of taking the course outweigh the cost.

e) Productivity needs to be improved at Acme Publishing Company.

Evidence needed:

a) The ability for employees to read faster is important to productivity at Acme Publishing Company.

b) The percentage of employees whose jobs require them to read rapidly.

c) The manner in which employees are promoted at Acme Publishing Company.

d) The focus of businesses that have seen greater productivity after their workers completed the speed-reading course.

e) The cost of travel for employees of Acme Publishing Company to travel and stay in Spruce City.

f) The effect on Acme Publishing Company of its employees' being gone for three weeks.

g) Other factors in addition to speed reading that led to the employee's promotion

h) Reading faster leads to greater knowledge.

i) The productivity of Acme workers.

After completing these steps, you should have enough material to write your analysis. Remember that you are not creating a position of your own; you are evaluating the strengths and weaknesses of the existing argument. You do not have to include all of the points that you have created in your prewriting. In fact, during the process of drafting your analysis, other ideas may come to mind, and, if they strengthen your analysis, you should include them.

Sample Essay

Companies are always looking for ways to improve the efficiency of their workers. Time is money, and the more that employees can accomplish in a workday, the more money the company is likely to make. Methods to increase productivity must be tailored to the type of work being done and the results desired by the company. Acme Publishing Company's owners need evidence of the benefit to be derived from the speed reading course before investing both time and money.

The ability to speed read is important in some occupations. Students doing research can benefit from quickly reading through documents in order to extract pertinent facts. Lawyers frequently wade through volumes of documents or case law, and the ability to speed read can save them a lot of time. Acme Publishing Company should determine how many of its employees actually need to read more quickly in order to perform more efficiently. The focus of the business may not include voluminous reading, so spending the money on the course for all of Acme's employees would not be a wise use of resources. Committing to a three-week retreat for all employees may be unrealistic. If the retreat is scheduled for only one three-week period, Acme Publishing Company would have to shut down to send all of its workers, potentially leading to a loss of business. The company may decide that some of its workers could become more productive after taking the speed-reading course and attending the retreat which would cost much less while, perhaps, making those employees feel more positive about their jobs.

The personnel manager cites examples of employees at one or more other companies who increased their reading speed or got promotions after taking the course. It would be helpful to know how rapidly the first employee read 500 pages before taking the course and whether or not reading faster was the main objective of his job. Evidence should also be forthcoming that the assistant manager's receiving a promotion was a direct result of taking the speed-reading course. That employee may have been in line to become vice president anyway based on his or her other qualifications. The president of Acme Publishing Company also needs evidence that the two employees cited work for a company whose goals and objectives are similar to those of Acme. If the other company involves vastly different work or product than Acme Publishing, then the examples are irrelevant. The ability to read rapidly may not be a factor in earning promotions at Acme Publishing. Evaluating the strength of this argument would be easier if the reader knows the criteria that Acme uses when selecting candidates for higher positions in the company.

Before accepting this recommendation, the company president should ask for evidence about his workers' level of productivity at all tasks required by Acme. The evidence may show that all of his workers meet established productivity levels, making the speed-reading course unnecessary. He may find that productivity levels are sub par in areas where the ability to read quickly is not a factor. On the other hand, he may find lower productivity in departments where a course in speed-reading would help those workers perform better. This evidence can help the president determine which of his personnel can help the Company move forward by completing the recommended course.

The president of Acme Publishing needs evidence that speed reading leads to the absorption of more knowledge. Because more knowledge is important in virtually every industry, this evidence could prove the value of the course to the company and its employees. Lack of this evidence negates the personnel director's conclusion that the money spent on the speed reading course would be a wise use of company resources.

Argument Task 10

The following appeared in a letter from the owner of the Sunnyside Towers apartment complex to its manager.

"One month ago, all the showerheads in the first three buildings of the Sunnyside Towers complex were modified to restrict maximum water flow to one-third of what it used to be. Although actual readings of water usage before and after the adjustment are not yet available, the change will obviously result in a considerable savings for Sunnyside Corporation, since the corporation must pay for water each month. Except for a few complaints about low water pressure, no problems with showers have been reported since the adjustment. Clearly, modifying showerheads to restrict water flow throughout all twelve buildings in the Sunnyside Towers complex will increase our profits further."

Write a response in which you discuss what specific evidence is needed to evaluate the argument and explain how the evidence would weaken or strengthen the argument.

Strategies

A good place to start your analysis is by creating a statement that reveals the main idea of the argument. Although the writer is creating an argument, he may ultimately be stating a position, making a recommendation, or making a prediction. It may be helpful for you to determine which of these formats is most evident in the argument.

The owner of Sunnyside Corporation is touting the money-saving benefits of installing low-flow shower heads in all of the units at Sunnyside Towers as a means of increasing profits.

Assumptions:

a) Water used for showers is a significant contributor to total water usage.

b) Residents will spend the same amount of time showering as they did before installation of the new shower heads.

c) Reducing water usage is the best way to increase profits.

d) Residents take showers rather than baths.

e) Residency rates and types will remain constant.

Evidence needed:

a) The portion of total water usage attributed to showering.

b) Water consumption before and after installation of the new shower heads.

c) How much time residents spend showering after installation of the new shower heads as opposed to time spent before doing so?

d) Occupancy rate in the three buildings with new shower heads.

e) Other steps the owner may have taken to save money.

f) How the owner determined that shower head replacement is a good way to save money?

g) If the owner pays any other utilities like heat or cable, etc.

h) How much water is used for other tasks, like laundry, dish washers, a pool?

i) Whether or not other costs of operation have increased.

j) The month during which the new shower heads were in use.

After completing these steps, you should have enough material to write your analysis. Remember that you are not creating a position of your own; you are evaluating the strengths and weaknesses of the existing argument. You do not have to include all of the points that you have created in your prewriting. In fact, during the process of drafting your analysis, other ideas may come to mind, and, if they strengthen your analysis, you should include them.

Sample Essay

Making a profit is the key to remaining in business. The owner of Sunnyside Towers has taken what he declares to be an important step to insuring the solvency of his business. Gathering more evidence about the cost of operations at Sunnyside Towers may lead the owner to decide he could have taken more or other steps to reduce expenses and increase profitability.

Of course, the most helpful piece of evidence, which the owner says is not yet available, is the water usage before and after installing the new shower heads. In the meantime, other evidence may shed light on the savings likely to be incurred by completing the conversion. The owner might begin by determining how much of the total water usage in the buildings is attributed to showers. Other appliances that use water include toilets, dishwashers, and washing machines. Knowing how much water the tenants use to complete these activities may lead the owner to seek savings in other areas. Some tenants may prefer baths to showers, so low-flow shower heads will have little impact in those apartments. In addition to household appliances, the owner may have installed a lawn sprinkler; the complex may have a pool. Those amenities might account for a great deal of total water usage in the complex. If the weather has been warmer and/or drier than normal, the sprinklers and pool may be used more than in an average year.

Another piece of evidence that would be helpful is a maintenance log. Each unit in the complex has a kitchen and at least one bathroom. If only half of them have leaky faucets, gallons of water are wasted every day. The owner may discover that repairing the faucets is more cost-effective both in materials and water saved. The maintenance log may also reveal that several steps, such as repairing leaky faucets, have already been taken and replacing the shower heads is the next logical step.

Knowing the occupancy rates in the buildings would help to evaluate the argument. Low occupancy in the three buildings that have had shower heads replaced might account for the low number of complaints about water pressure. It would be helpful to know if those complainants are taking longer showers to compensate for the reduction in pressure. Full occupancy might lead to more complaints. In fact, knowing the occupancy rates of all twelve buildings would help to make decisions about changes that increase profitability. If several apartments in each building are empty, replacing the shower heads is not likely to have much impact on profits. If most units are full, however, the savings realized from each shower head will be multiplied.

Evidence relating to all operating expenses will help determine what changes, if any, should be made at the apartment complex to increase profits. If the owner pays for heat as well as water, he has likely seen an increase in the cost of doing so. Oil prices have risen, and the owner may find greater savings by turning down the thermostats a couple of degrees or adding insulation to the walls. The cost to mow the lawns or plow the driveways may have risen. Without investigating all costs associated with the apartment buildings, the owner may discover that the money he saves on water usage is offset by greater expenditures in other areas.

Knowing which month the shower heads were in use would help to evaluate the argument. If it was a winter month, overall water usage may be less because sprinklers are idle. During the summer, several residents may be away on vacation, so water used for showers would be reduced. Evidence about rainfall totals and frequency may help him decide to change or reduce the amount of time that the sprinklers are in operation.

Attributing savings to shower heads may be incorrect. In fact, any savings or extra expenditures at any time of the year may be difficult to credit to the installation of the shower heads unless some of the water meters for the complex are dedicated to measuring water used for showering. The owner of Sunnyside Towers needs more evidence about water usage before declaring that new shower heads will create a significant savings.

Argument Task 11

The following appeared in a letter to the school board in the town of Centerville.

"All students should be required to take the driver's education course at Centerville High School. In the past two years, several accidents in and around Centerville have involved teenage drivers. Since a number of parents in Centerville have complained that they are too busy to teach their teenagers to drive, some other instruction is necessary to ensure that these teenagers are safe drivers. Although there are two driving schools in Centerville, parents on a tight budget cannot afford to pay for driving instruction. Therefore an effective and mandatory program sponsored by the high school is the only solution to this serious problem."

Write a response in which you examine the stated and/or unstated assumptions of the argument. Be sure to explain how the argument depends on these assumptions and what the implications are for the argument if the assumptions prove unwarranted.

Strategies

A good place to start your analysis is by creating a statement that reveals the main idea of the argument. Although the writer is creating an argument, he may ultimately be stating a position, making a recommendation, or making a prediction. It may be helpful for you to determine which of these formats is most evident in the argument.

The author of the letter to the Centerville school board uses some information regarding teenage drivers and accidents to recommend a mandatory driver education course at the local high school.

Assumptions:

a) Teenage drivers caused all of the accidents in which they were involved.

b) A school-sponsored driver education course is the only way to ensure that teens are safe drivers.

c) Accidents involving teen drivers are a serious problem.

d) The school-sponsored course can accommodate all students.

e) Driver inexperience is the cause of most accidents.

f) All teens want to learn to drive.

g) Teens are worse drivers than those in other age groups.

h) Parents are too busy to teach their teens to drive.

i) Driving schools are too expensive.

Alternative explanations:

a) Teens are not always at fault when involved in an accident.

b) A small percentage of total accidents involve teen drivers.

c) The school system cannot accommodate all students who wish to take the driving course.

d) Distracted driving is the cause of most accidents.

e) There has been considerable road construction during the past two years.

f) Elderly drivers cause as many or more accidents than teens.

g) Adopting a graduated driver's license program is an effective way to reduce accidents by teen drivers.

After completing these steps, you should have enough material to write your analysis. Remember that you are not creating a position of your own; you are evaluating the strengths and weaknesses of the existing argument. You do not have to include all of the points that you have created in your prewriting. In fact, during the process of drafting your analysis, other ideas may come to mind, and, if they strengthen your analysis, you should include them.

Sample Essay

Teenage driving is a frequent topic of discussion with parents, other authorities and insurance companies. Teen drivers in small towns know that the local cops are more likely to stop them than other drivers. These drivers know that they or their parents pay higher insurance premiums than do other drivers. One can only assume that teen drivers pose higher risks or drive less prudently than other drivers. Compelling all students at Centerville High School to take a driver education course through the school may not be the only or best way to reduce the number of accidents in the surrounding area.

The assumption that teens cause all of the accidents in which they are involved may be false. Even though teens are involved in an accident, the fault may be the other driver's. Even if each accident involving a teen driver is the teen's fault, the reader should not assume that they are a large portion of total accidents. Accidents caused by teen drivers may not result in serious injuries or extensive damage to cars or other property. During the two-year period mentioned in the argument, considerable road construction in the Centerville vicinity may have caused hazardous conditions for all drivers, so more accidents by all drivers occurred. The weather during this time span may have caused more dangerous driving conditions leading to a larger number of accidents involving teens and other drivers.

The author of the letter assumes that a mandatory driving course sponsored by the local high school is the only way to ensure that all teens learn to drive safely. There is no evidence that a high school course is more effective than other driving instruction for creating safe drivers. Requiring all students to take the course may be problematic. Some students may not be able to fit it into already challenging schedules. Some may not be interested in learning to drive. Many states have taken steps beyond driver education to reduce the number of accidents caused by teens. Some restrict new drivers to operating a vehicle only during daylight hours for the first six months. Others prohibit the teen driver from carrying passengers other than adults with licenses. These steps may be more effective in creating safer drivers than a mandatory course in high school.

The content of the letter leads to the assumption that teens are the worst divers on the road and that inexperience is the reason. Factors besides age influence a driver's ability to be safe. Good hearing and eyesight along with rapid reaction time keep drivers and others safe on our streets. Since it is the elderly drivers who may have poor vision and/

or reaction time, they may be the cause of as many accidents as teens are. Today, it is just as likely that a driver is distracted rather than inexperienced. More drivers of every age are using cell phones while operating a motor vehicle.

The conclusion that a high school course is the best solution is based in part on the assumptions that too many parents have no time to teach their teens to drive and that many families cannot afford the cost of the private driving schools. It would be helpful if the school board were given concrete numbers to support these assumptions. The number may be small enough to be significant; dedicating funds for the driver education course could put other programs at the school in jeopardy.

Drivers at any age can have accidents. Although experience prevents more serious accidents, other factors contribute to safety on the roads for everyone. Parents might be advised to buy the safest cars possible for their teens. Cars today have rear cameras that let drivers know of any obstacle behind them when they are backing up. Air bags save lives every day. When all of the factors are considered, the school board may decide that a course at the high school is the best decision, but they also may determine that other options are just as viable for creating safe, young drivers.

Argument Task 12

The following appeared in a memo from a budget planner for the city of Grandview.

"Our citizens are well aware of the fact that while the Grandview Symphony Orchestra was struggling to succeed, our city government promised annual funding to help support its programs. Last year, however, private contributions to the symphony increased by 200 percent, and attendance at the symphony's concerts-in-the-park series doubled. The symphony has also announced an increase in ticket prices for next year. Such developments indicate that the symphony can now succeed without funding from city government and we can eliminate that expense from next year's budget. Therefore, we recommend that the city of Grandview eliminate its funding for the Grandview Symphony from next year's budget. By doing so, we can prevent a city budget deficit without threatening the success of the symphony."

Write a response in which you discuss what questions would need to be answered in order to decide whether the recommendation is likely to have the predicted result. Be sure to explain how the answers to these questions would help to evaluate the recommendation.

Strategies

A good place to start your analysis is by creating a statement that reveals the main idea of the argument. Although the writer is creating an argument, he may ultimately be stating a position, making a recommendation, or making a prediction. It may be helpful for you to determine which of these formats is most evident in the argument.

Based on information about new revenues for the Grandview Symphony Orchestra, the budget planner for Grandview concludes that the city can eliminate its traditional funding of the orchestra and avoid a budget deficit.

Assumptions:

a) Increased donations and higher ticket prices will enable the Grandview Symphony Orchestra to function without funding from the city.

b) Those who attended concerts in the park will pay to attend regular performances.

c) Eliminating funding for the symphony will prevent a budget deficit.

d) People will pay higher prices for tickets.

e) Private donations will remain at the increased level.

f) Avoiding a budget deficit relies on eliminating funding for the symphony orchestra.

Questions:

a) What percentage of the symphony's expenses is covered by private donations?

b) What percentage of the symphony's expenses is covered by ticket sales?

c) How will an increase in ticket prices affect sales?

d) What was the total of private donations prior to the increase?

e) How much money is raised by the concerts in the park?

f) What portion of the city budget is dedicated to the symphony orchestra?

g) How important is the orchestra to the city?

After completing these steps, you should have enough material to write your analysis. Remember that you are not creating a position of your own; you are evaluating the strengths and weaknesses of the existing argument. You do not have to include all of the points that you have created in your prewriting. In fact, during the process of drafting your analysis, other ideas may come to mind, and, if they strengthen your analysis, you should include them.

Sample Essay

Cities are responsible for allocating tax dollars to institutions and services that provide the most benefit for their citizens. They fund police and fire departments, schools, and public works. They may also contribute to libraries, recreation departments, and museums. When budgets are tight, those in control may have to decide between repairing the streets and putting a new roof on the library. They may ask the school department to eliminate positions or public works to cancel overtime. Grandview's budget planner appears to have sufficient evidence that demonstrates the likelihood of continued success for the Grandview Symphony Orchestra. He predicts that the city can eliminate its usual funding of the orchestra and, thus, avoid a budget deficit. The strength of his prediction relies on the answers to several questions.

What portion of the orchestra's budget comes from the various sources? First, consider the city's contribution. If it is a small portion, losing the money may not have any impact on the ability of the orchestra to survive. On the other hand, if it is a large portion of the orchestra's operating budget, losing it, even with the increase in donations and higher ticket prices, may cause the orchestra to fail. Second is the portion provided by private donations. The size of it determines whether or not a 200 percent increase is significant. If private patrons formerly supplied 10 percent of the orchestra's budget, the increase would represent a current 30 percent of the budget. That increase alone may enable the orchestra to survive easily without a contribution from the city. In contrast, private money that formerly constituted only two percent of the total operating budget, would now be six percent, which may still leave the orchestra in need of city money. It would appear that the increase in donations is insufficient to ensure the financial health of the orchestra. Ticket prices also contribute to the orchestra's finances, and the group has plans to increase them. What effect will higher prices have on ticket sales? Lower sales could offset any gains made by increased prices. How many people attended the concerts in the park before the audience doubled in size, and did they pay an admission fee? Doubling becomes more meaningful the higher the base number is. If that audience paid no admission fee, the number of people in it doesn't matter because the series is not a source of revenue for the orchestra. In fact, people who can attend free concerts in the park may forego buying tickets for an inside performance, dismissing the revenue stream for the orchestra.

How important is the orchestra to the city? The Grandview City Orchestra may be a highly regarded institution that brings people to the city from surrounding towns. They may have dinner in local restaurants before the performance.

Some may travel from far away and need to stay in a hotel. The revenue generated by concert goers may more than offset the orchestra's cost to the city.

What portion of the city budget is dedicated to the symphony orchestra? Is it a large enough expenditure that eliminating it will make a significant difference in the city's budget? The actual contribution by the city may be a fraction of one percent of the total budget. Depending on the size of the forecasted deficit, the money given to the orchestra may make little difference, or it may be just enough to prevent the deficit.

What happens if the orchestra falls on hard times in the future? Will the city be able to reinstate its contribution, or will the symphony orchestra be forced to shut down? If this should occur a few years down the road, the city may have committed the funds it formerly gave to the city orchestra to some other facility in the city. The likelihood of the city's finding that money again is slim. The orchestra may leave behind an empty building that will be difficult to sell and, thus, create an unattractive appearance in its neighborhood.

Too many questions are left to be answered before the city leaders make what may be an unwise and irrevocable decision about the future of the Grandview City Orchestra. When they have sufficient information, the council or mayor can make a more informed choice about the funding. The predicted result of avoiding a budget deficit by not funding the orchestra may be proven false.

Argument Task 13

The following appeared in a letter from a firm providing investment advice to a client.

"Homes in the northeastern United States, where winters are typically cold, have traditionally used oil as their major fuel for heating. Last year that region experienced 90 days with below-average temperatures, and climate forecasters at Waymarsh University predict that this weather pattern will continue for several more years. Furthermore, many new homes have been built in this region during the past year. Because these developments will certainly result in an increased demand for heating oil, we recommend investment in Consolidated Industries, one of whose major business operations is the retail sale of home heating oil."

Write a response in which you discuss what questions would need to be answered in order to decide whether the recommendation and the argument on which it is based are reasonable. Be sure to explain how the answers to these questions would help to evaluate the recommendation.

Strategies

A good place to start your analysis is by creating a statement that reveals the main idea of the argument. Although the writer is creating an argument, he may ultimately be stating a position, making a recommendation, or making a prediction. It may be helpful for you to determine which of these formats is most evident in the argument.

An investment firm is recommending that a client invest in Consolidated Industries based on the predicted use of heating fuel in new homes being built in the northeastern United States.

Assumptions:

a) Newly constructed homes will heat with oil.

b) Below-average temperatures will continue for several years.

c) The price for home heating oil will remain high.

d) Oil is a significant portion of Consolidated Industries' holdings.

e) Profits from the oil business will offset any potential losses in other Consolidated Industries' holdings.

Questions:

a) What portion of Consolidated Industries business is oil?

b) What type of heating systems have been installed in the new-construction homes?

c) How far below-average were the temperatures last year?

d) How have investments in Consolidated Industries performed in the past?

e) What are the client's investment goals?

f) Has the company's advice paid off in the past?

g) Does the client have the money to make the investment?

After completing these steps, you should have enough material to write your analysis. Remember that you are not creating a position of your own; you are evaluating the strengths and weaknesses of the existing argument. You do not have to include all of the points that you have created in your prewriting. In fact, during the process of drafting your analysis, other ideas may come to mind, and, if they strengthen your analysis, you should include them.

Sample Essay

The average working man or woman has too little time or knowledge to navigate the ins and outs of the stock market, and most rely on the advice of a financial planner. It is easier to simply put one's money where the planner recommends. The smart investor asks questions, and he or she should before buying stock in Consolidated Industries. The answers to those questions will lead the investor to agree with the planner or decide to dive into another industry altogether.

The investment adviser assumes that new homes built in the northeast will use oil for heat. Are other types of heating systems becoming more prevalent? The rising cost of heating fuel has led homeowners to supplement oil with pellet stoves or heat pumps or, perhaps even solar panels. Builders of new homes may have to install these in order to appeal to modern consumers, many of whom want to reduce this country's dependence on foreign oil.

Have the home builders taken any other steps to reduce heating costs? They may have oriented the homes to take advantage of passive solar heat so that, on sunny days, the rooms where families spend most of their time will be warmed by the sun, reducing the number of hours that homeowners will need to run the furnace. Builders are able to select from a variety of components that reduce energy consumption. Double-pane, low-E windows prevent heat from escaping the house in the winter; a variety of insulating materials keep cold air out.

How far below average were the temperatures last year, and did those days occur during the winter? If those days were one degree below average, they did not make a significant contribution to heating costs. If a chunk of those days occurred during the summer months, they probably had little impact on oil consumption. If they occurred during the winter months and were several degrees below average, they would have increased the amount of time that homeowners turned their furnaces up, causing more gallons of fuel to be burned.

In addition to answers about the likelihood of increased oil sales in the northeast, the investor needs answers to questions about Consolidated Industries itself. How big a portion of the company's holdings are in heating fuel? Even though the financial planner cites heating oil as one of Consolidated's major holdings, he may have failed to mention that it is one of many major industries in which Consolidated has an interest. How is Consolidated Industries performing overall? Even though its oil division may be very profitable, its other holdings may be under performing, making an investment in Consolidated an unwise decision. In contrast, Consolidated's other holdings may be profitable enough to make it a sound investment even if heating oil experiences either a dip in price or a decline in consumption.

Once this client has answers to these questions, he or she can make a more informed decision about the investment. Before jumping on board this investor should also consider how his advisor has performed for him or her in the past and how an investment in Consolidated Industries fits with the other stocks in his or her portfolio. How does this investment help or hinder the client's financial goals? Will it help him send his children to college or make possible an earlier, more comfortable retirement? The client may want a rapid return in order to meet some short-term goals. Does the client even have the necessary funds to invest? He may have other commitments to meet at present. If the answers are satisfying, he should hand his money over to the financial planner.

Argument Task 14

The following appeared in a memo from the marketing director of Top Dog Pet Stores.

"Five years ago Fish Emporium started advertising in the magazine Exotic Pets Monthly. Their stores saw sales increase by 15 percent after their ads began appearing in the magazine. The three Fish Emporium stores in Gulf City saw an even greater increase than that. Because Top Dog Pet Stores is based in Gulf City, it seems clear that we should start placing our own ads in Exotic Pets Monthly. If we do so, we will be sure to reverse the recent trend of declining sales and start making a profit again."

Write a response in which you examine the stated and/or unstated assumptions of the argument. Be sure to explain how the argument depends on these assumptions and what the implications are for the argument if the assumptions prove unwarranted.

Strategies

A good place to start your analysis is by creating a statement that reveals the main idea of the argument. Although the writer is creating an argument, he may ultimately be stating a position, making a recommendation, or making a prediction. It may be helpful for you to determine which of these formats is most evident in the argument.

Based on an increase in sales for Fish Emporium after it advertised in Exotic Pets Monthly, the marketing director of Top Dog Pet Stores recommends that they advertise in the same publication in order to make the business profitable again.

Assumptions:

a) Advertising in Exotic Pets Monthly will increase sales for Top Dog Pet Stores.

b) Fish Emporium continues to experience higher sales.

c) Fish Emporium sales increased as a direct result of placing ads in Exotic Pets Monthly.

d) The increase in Fish Emporium sales in Gulf City stores was significantly higher than the 15% increase in their other stores.

e) Failure to advertise in Exotic Pets Monthly is the reason for declining sales and lack of profit for Top Dog Pet Stores.

f) All Top Dog Pet Stores have declining sales and profits.

Alternative explanations:

a) After the first rise in sales, Fish Emporium's sales have remained flat.

b) Fish Emporium made other changes at the same time that they began advertising in Exotic Pets Monthly.

c) The additional increase in profits in Fish Emporium's Gulf City stores was too small to be significant.

d) Top Dog Pet Stores may have made decisions or taken action that has resulted in a decline in sales.

e) Some Top Dog Pet Stores are profitable.

After completing these steps, you should have enough material to write your analysis. Remember that you are not creating a position of your own; you are evaluating the strengths and weaknesses of the existing argument. You do not have to include all of the points that you have created in your prewriting. In fact, during the process of drafting your analysis, other ideas may come to mind, and, if they strengthen your analysis, you should include them.

Sample Essay

The owner of Top Dog Pet Stores has created some assumptions about Fish Emporium's increase in sales that he believes apply to his own business. He should examine his assumptions to ensure that no other explanations for the increased sales exist before taking actions that may be costly and ineffective.

The owner of Top Dog Pet stores assumes that Fish Emporium increased its sales by placing ads in Exotic Pets Monthly. In fact, Fish Emporium may have made some other changes at the same time that are the real reason for greater sales. The owner may have added new products that are in high demand. They may have rearranged their displays to make higher priced goods more visible. Perhaps they cleaned up the store or hired more knowledgeable employees who made it easier for customers to find everything they need. In contrast, Top Dog Pet Stores may have failed to take similar actions to improve sales. The stores may be dirty, stocked with old or outdated merchandise, and manned by associates who have little knowledge about the products in the stores. In that case, no amount of advertising in any publication is likely to have any lasting positive effect on Top Dog's sales or profits.

The first rule of real estate is "location, location, location". The same is very often true in business. Customers must be able to find the store and park nearby. Fish Emporium's stores may be in ideal locations in Gulf City. They may be in popular malls or busy downtown shopping areas with plenty of free parking. Top Dog Pet Stores might be off the beaten path, making it difficult for customers to find them. The owner of Top Dog Pet Stores assumes that Gulf City is an ideal location for improving his business, and he bases his belief on the apparent success of Fish Emporium. Fish Emporium may have saturated the pet store market in Gulf City making Top Dog's success unlikely at best.

A 15 percent increase in sales sounds significant. Whether or not it is depends on what sales were when Fish Emporium began its advertising campaign in Exotic Pets Monthly. The owner of Top Dog Pet Stores may assume that the increase is on top of already satisfactory sales. If sales had fallen to an all-time low before the advertising campaign, the increase may have simply returned sales to previous levels. However, if sales were good prior to the ads, then the increase is something to celebrate. The even greater increase in sales at the Gulf City stores might be minor, in which case, Top Dog should not base its decision to run a similar campaign on that increase. Fish Emporium could have run a special promotion when it advertised in the magazine, attracting new customers and leading to a temporary up tick in sales. They may not have sustained the increase over the five-year time span even though the argument may lead to that assumption.

The reader may assume that all Top Dog Pet Stores are experiencing a decline in sales and profits. Companies with stores in different locations are servants to the vagaries of the marketplace. Some stores may be located in towns that are experiencing an economic downturn, and people cannot afford to spend money on pets and pet supplies. In contrast, other stores may be located in towns or cities where the economy is booming and residents have the discretionary income to spend on treats for their pets. The owners may be better off by advertising in local newspapers or on local radio and television stations where sales have fallen off. Tailoring its advertising for each location may be a better strategy than relying on one outlet for its promotions.

It is common to assume that the steps to success for one business apply to all businesses or, at least, all similar businesses. This assumption can lead to costly mistakes. All conditions should be examined before spending money on any advertising.

Argument Task 15

The following memo appeared in the newsletter of the West Meria Public Health Council.

"An innovative treatment has come to our attention that promises to significantly reduce absenteeism in our schools and workplaces. A study reports that in nearby East Meria, where fish consumption is very high, people visit the doctor only once or twice per year for the treatment of colds. This shows that eating a substantial amount of fish can clearly prevent colds. Furthermore, since colds are the reason most frequently given for absences from school and work, attendance levels will improve. Therefore, we recommend the daily use of a nutritional supplement derived from fish oil as a good way to prevent colds and lower absenteeism."

Write a response in which you discuss what questions would need to be answered in order to decide whether the recommendation and the argument on which it is based are reasonable. Be sure to explain how the answers to these questions would help to evaluate the recommendation.

NOTE: The above topic has wording similar to Agrument Task 24 of GRE Analytical Writing Solutions to the Real Essay Topics - Book 1. However, if you read carefully you will notice that the task instructions are different. Hence, it is very important to read the topic as well as its instructions completely before you start to write your response.

Strategies

A good place to start your analysis is by creating a statement that reveals the main idea of the argument. Although the writer is creating an argument, he may ultimately be stating a position, making a recommendation, or making a prediction. It may be helpful for you to determine which of these formats is most evident in the argument.

The West Meria Public Health Council uses the low-frequency of doctor visits by residents of East Meria to support its recommendation that West Merians take a fish oil supplement.

Assumptions:

a) High fish consumption in East Meria leads to fewer visits to the doctor for treatment of colds.

b) Fewer colds will increase attendance at work and school.

c) People always see a doctor for treatment of colds.

d) A daily nutritional supplement from fish oil will have the same effect as eating fish.

e) People are truthful about their reasons for missing school or work.

f) People will willingly and consistently take the supplement.

g) People in West Meria eat less fish than people in East Meria.

Questions:

a) Does everyone see a doctor for treatment of every cold?

b) Do citizens who eat the most fish have the fewest colds?

c) Do residents of East Meria take any other steps to prevent colds?

d) Are residents truthful with their employers about their reasons for missing work?

e) Have East Meria's schools and workplaces seen a significant decline in absenteeism?

f) Is the supplement affordable?

g) How significant a problem is absenteeism in West Meria?

h) Do East Merians have easy access to doctors?

i) Do citizens of East Meria eat significantly more fish than those in West Meria?

After completing these steps, you should have enough material to write your analysis. Remember that you are not creating a position of your own; you are evaluating the strengths and weaknesses of the existing argument. You do not have to include all of the points that you have created in your prewriting. In fact, during the process of drafting your analysis, other ideas may come to mind, and, if they strengthen your analysis, you should include them.

Sample Essay

The recommendation in this argument lacks sufficient support. A number of questions need answers before deciding on the efficacy of the recommendation that citizens of West Meria take a fish oil supplement each day in order to reduce the incidence of colds and improve attendance at work and school.

The first questions should attempt to clarify the reason for the implication that East Meria residents have fewer colds. Do they really have fewer colds or do they simply seek treatment less often than residents of West Meria? If a survey of East Meria residents shows that they do, indeed, have significantly fewer colds than people in West Meria, further investigation of lifestyle choices is warranted. On the other hand, survey results showing that they simply choose not to seek treatment for colds as often as people in West Meria invalidate the claim that eating fish makes East Meria residents less susceptible to colds.

Do East Meria residents take any other action that might result in fewer colds? They may avoid smoking tobacco, since smoking is linked to a variety of upper-respiratory illnesses. Perhaps they take daily supplements like Vitamin C or Echinacea, both of which purport to boost the immune system. East Merians may exercise regularly and maintain ideal weights. If any of these conditions exist, the argument and concomitant recommendation become weaker.

One may infer from the argument that absenteeism is a big problem in West Meria, but is that the case? It is likely that people suffer colds more frequently than any other illness, but many go to work or school in spite of them. Without asking schools and businesses about their rates of absenteeism, it is impossible to determine the benefits of taking the fish oil supplement. Do workers and students in East Meria miss fewer days of work or school than residents of West Meria? Visiting the doctor fewer times each year does not necessarily indicate that East Merians have less absenteeism. In fact, residents of East Meria may contract more serious illnesses than do citizens of West Meria. Has the West Meria Public Health Council collected data on all types of illnesses?

How likely are West Merians to take the supplement? It may be too expensive or difficult to obtain. If they are not currently taking any action to avoid catching colds, they may balk at taking the supplement. Is there research that proves taking the supplement is effective in boosting the immune system? Residents may want to know how effective the supplement is before laying down any amount of money to purchase it.

Why is fish consumption so high in East Meria? Commercial fishing may be the main industry there, making easy access to fresh fish and prices low enough to make fish the protein of choice. Do East Merians in fact eat considerably more fish than West Merians? Residents of both towns may consume equal amounts of fish. What, then accounts for the higher number of doctor visits in West Meria? They may have better health insurance that pays for those doctor visits. The citizens of East Meria may have to pay for doctor visits out-of-pocket and cannot afford to do so every time one has a cold.

Do colds account for the greatest number of absentee days? Although colds may be the most common reason for missing work or school, those suffering from them may miss only a day or two, whereas a more serious illness may require a longer absence from work. Are people always truthful about the reason they give for missing work? It's easier for people to say they have a cold than to admit they are hung-over or simply need a "mental health" day.

Until the citizens of West Meria have answers to the questions about the efficacy of a supplement derived from fish oil as a cold preventive or the impact of colds compared to other illnesses on absenteeism, they cannot commit to buying and taking a daily supplement.

Argument Task 16

The following appeared in a memo from the vice president of a company that builds shopping malls around the country.

"The surface of a section of Route 101, paved just two years ago by Good Intentions Roadways, is now badly cracked with a number of dangerous potholes. In another part of the state, a section of Route 40, paved by Appian Roadways more than four years ago, is still in good condition. In a demonstration of their continuing commitment to quality, Appian Roadways recently purchased state-of-the-art paving machinery and hired a new quality-control manager. Therefore, I recommend hiring Appian Roadways to construct the access roads for all our new shopping malls. I predict that our Appian access roads will not have to be repaired for at least four years."

Write a response in which you discuss what questions would need to be answered in order to decide whether the recommendation is likely to have the predicted result. Be sure to explain how the answers to these questions would help to evaluate the recommendation.

Strategies

A good place to start your analysis is by creating a statement that reveals the main idea of the argument. Although the writer is creating an argument, he may ultimately be stating a position, making a recommendation, or making a prediction. It may be helpful for you to determine which of these formats is most evident in the argument.

The writer argues that Appian Roadways will be a better choice than Good Intentions Roadways for paving the access roads to his new shopping malls and predicts that the pavement should remain free of repairs for at least four years.

Assumptions:

a) Routes 101 and 40 handle the same amount and type of traffic.

b) Both routes have the same type of pavement.

c) Mall access roads will experience the same traffic conditions as Route 40.

d) New machinery guarantees good work.

e) Weather conditions are identical in both parts of the state.

f) Appian Roadways does better work than Good Intentions Roadways.

g) Good Intentions Roadways uses outdated equipment.

Questions:

a) How does the traffic on Route 101 compare to the traffic on Route 40?

b) Are weather conditions the same in both parts of the state?

c) Why did Appian Way buy new equipment?

d) Does Appian Way's paving generally last longer than that of other companies?

e) How has Good Intentions performed on other paving projects?

f) Are the malls in question located in various parts of the state?

After completing these steps, you should have enough material to write your analysis. Remember that you are not creating a position of your own; you are evaluating the strengths and weaknesses of the existing argument. You do not have to include all of the points that you have created in your prewriting. In fact, during the process of drafting your analysis, other ideas may come to mind, and, if they strengthen your analysis, you should include them.

Sample Essay

This argument reveals information that makes it appear that Appian Way provides road paving that lasts longer than that of Good Intentions Roadways. All things being equal, that may be true. The scant information in this argument raises several questions that must be answered before selecting a paving contractor, and the mall developer may discover inequities that affect his decision.

Are weather conditions the same in both parts of the state mentioned in the argument? Many states are large enough or varied enough in geography to experience varied weather conditions at any time of the year. Northern parts of the state may have a long winter season leading to frost heaves which crack the pavement in the spring. Warmer parts of the state may have large amounts of rain that cause washouts and undermining of the pavement. Has there been any unusually severe weather event along Route 101 during the past two years that could account for its state of disrepair? A hurricane or tornado could have caused more-than-normal wear on a stretch of highway. Route 101 may follow the winding course of a river or curve around geographical formations such as mountains causing more rapid wear and tear on the pavement. In contrast, Route 40 may pass through a portion of the state where the average temperature is moderate and no geographical impediments stand in the way of the road's running flat and straight.

Is traffic different on both roadways? The volume of traffic on Route 101 might be considerably higher than the volume of traffic on Route 40. Even if the number of vehicles along both highways may be the same, the types of vehicles traveling on each may affect the durability of each road's surface. Large numbers of heavy trucks can cause more wear and tear on a road's surface in a shorter period of time than the same number of passenger vehicles. Concerns about the efficacy of one paving company over the other can be allayed by answering these questions.

Why did Appian Way buy new equipment? Does the company regularly update to the newest equipment? A company that demonstrates careful attention to quality by updating its equipment is an attractive choice on the surface. On the other hand, a company that allows its equipment to fall into disrepair and must replace it may have the same negligent attitude toward the work it does. Does Good Intentions also have the latest equipment? If so, the state of either company's equipment is not a sufficient reason to choose one over the other. One should also ask why Appian Way has hired a new quality-control manager. Has Appian Way received complaints about the quality of their work? The nature of the work done on Route 40 may not be typical of the company's paving ability. Likewise, the sub par work on Route 101 may not be representative of the quality that Good Intentions normally produces. How has each company performed over time? Knowing that one or the other of the paving concerns has an exemplary record for quality and durability would help the mall developers choose the best candidate for their projects.

Are the malls in question located in various parts of the state? Depending on their locations, the malls may be subject to traffic and weather conditions that will affect the durability of the paving on their access roads. Predicting that Appian Way's paving will not need repair for at least four years may be overly optimistic. Adopting the recommendation and accepting the prediction that follows should be done only after answering several questions.

Argument Task 17

A recent sales study indicates that consumption of seafood dishes in Bay City restaurants has increased by 30 percent during the past five years. Yet there are no currently operating city restaurants whose specialty is seafood. Moreover, the majority of families in Bay City are two-income families, and a nationwide study has shown that such families eat significantly fewer home-cooked meals than they did a decade ago but at the same time express more concern about healthful eating. Therefore, the new Captain Seafood restaurant that specializes in seafood should be quite popular and profitable.

Write a response in which you discuss what questions would need to be addressed in order to decide whether the conclusion and the argument on which it is based are reasonable. Be sure to explain how the answers to the questions would help to evaluate the conclusion.

NOTE: The above topic has wording similar toAgrument Task 27 of GRE Analytical Writing Solutions to the Real Essay Topics - Book 1. However, if you read carefully you will notice that the task instructions are different. Hence, it is very important to read the topic as well as its instructions completely before you start to write your response.

Strategies

A good place to start your analysis is by creating a statement that reveals the main idea of the argument. Although the writer is creating an argument, he may ultimately be stating a position, making a recommendation, or making a prediction. It may be helpful for you to determine which of these formats is most evident in the argument.

The author predicts that a new Captain Seafood restaurant in Bay City should be very profitable based on an apparent increase in the consumption of seafood dishes at local restaurants.

Assumptions:

a) Seafood dishes are healthier than other types of entrees.

b) A seafood restaurant will be successful in Bay City.

c) All restaurants in Bay City have seen a 30 percent increase in the sales of seafood dishes.

d) A 30 percent increase in the consumption of seafood dishes is significant.

e) Restaurants in Bay City are selling fewer meat and poultry entrees.

Questions:

a) Have seafood restaurants opened and closed in Bay City?

b) Do seafood dishes generate as much profit as meat and poultry dishes?

c) Is a 30 percent increase in the consumption of seafood dishes significant?

d) What percentage of total sales is represented by seafood dishes?

e) Are seafood dishes inherently healthier than other meat dishes?

After completing these steps, you should have enough material to write your analysis. Remember that you are not creating a position of your own; you are evaluating the strengths and weaknesses of the existing argument. You do not have to include all of the points that you have created in your prewriting. In fact, during the process of drafting your analysis, other ideas may come to mind, and, if they strengthen your analysis, you should include them.

Sample Essay

Anyone relying on the conclusion in this argument should first seek answers to several questions before conceding that the new Captain Seafood restaurant will be successful in Bay City. Any restaurateur needs more details about the facts offered in this scant list of reasons that support the promise of profitability in serving seafood to the residents of the town.

The survey reveals that consumption of seafood dishes in Bay City restaurants has increased by 30 percent during the past five years. The percentage is significant, but how does that translate into dollars? For example, suppose that sales of seafood dishes five years ago totaled $500. A 30 percent increase would mean that the most recent sales total $650. On the other hand, sales of $50,000 five years ago would be $65,000 today. Determining the success of the new Captain Seafood eatery based on an increase in sales would depend on which answer is correct. The significance of the increase would also depend on how high or low the percentage of sales was in previous years. What was the percentage of sales represented by seafood dishes? If it were 5 percent, a 30 percent increase would mean that current sales are 6 1/2 percent, hardly enough to declare that Captain Seafood will be profitable. If previous sales accounted for 20 percent of total sales, today they are 26 percent of the total. Now one in four orders is for seafood dishes, perhaps a significant number to make the author's conclusion reasonable.

Does an increase in the sales of seafood dishes translate into higher profits? If, for example, the restaurant serves lobster, it must have a tank in which to keep those crustaceans alive. Some are likely to die anyway, and they must be discarded, and those sales are lost. Seafood tends to be more delicate in nature than beef, pork, or chicken and may require more labor-intensive handling and preparation which increases overhead. Pricing seafood dishes to make them as attractive as other entrees may have a negative effect on the bottom line.

Why are there no seafood restaurants currently operating in Bay City? The use of the word currently, itself, may give pause to anyone considering this enterprise in the city. If such restaurants existed in the past, one should seek to know why they closed. If they closed as a result of poor management, developing a strong business plan should, indeed, enable a restaurateur to presume success in a new venture. If, however, those restaurants closed because the citizens were not interested in seafood or could not afford the dishes, the start-up might not be a good idea. Relying on past restaurant's success rates may not be sufficient for making a decision. Have the demographics of Bay City changed significantly? The age and socioeconomic status of Bay City residents may have risen or declined. If the average age is lower and the median income higher, families may have more expendable income to spend on dining out and ordering what may be pricier seafood entrees. On the other hand, an elderly population with a lower median income creates more risk for the new Captain Seafood restaurant.

Are seafood dishes more suitable for a health-conscious diet than other types of dishes? Before using this rationale to predict success for a seafood restaurant in Bay City, one must also ask what method has been used to prepare the most popular dishes in the local restaurants. If battered, deep-fried fish and clams are the most frequently ordered main courses, the impetus to order them is unlikely to be reduced fat and calories. Conversely, if the most popular dishes are steamed or poached fish fillets, the question may be answered in the affirmative.

The answers to these questions should help to evaluate the author's prediction of success for Captain Seafood in Bay City. Relying solely on the insufficient and, perhaps, anecdotal information in the argument might lead the reader to an erroneous conclusion about the likelihood of the new restaurant's ability to thrive.

Argument Task 18

The following appeared in a memo from the director of student housing at Buckingham College.

"To serve the housing needs of our students, Buckingham College should build a number of new dormitories. Buckingham's enrollment is growing and, based on current trends, will double over the next 50 years, thus making existing dormitory space inadequate. Moreover, the average rent for an apartment in our town has risen in recent years. Consequently, students will find it increasingly difficult to afford off-campus housing. Finally, attractive new dormitories would make prospective students more likely to enroll at Buckingham."

Write a response in which you discuss what specific evidence is needed to evaluate the argument and explain how the evidence would weaken or strengthen the argument.

Strategies

A good place to start your analysis is by creating a statement that reveals the main idea of the argument. Although the writer is creating an argument, he may ultimately be stating a position, making a recommendation, or making a prediction. It may be helpful for you to determine which of these formats is most evident in the argument.

The housing director at Buckingham College recommends that the college build new dormitories to accommodate a projected growth in enrollment, make housing more affordable for students and to attract more students.

Assumptions:

a) A large number of future students at Buckingham College will choose to live in dormitories.

b) Living in dormitories is less expensive than renting apartments.

c) Buckingham College enrollment will continue to grow at its current rate.

d) Students select a college based on the attractiveness of its dorms.

e) Existing dorms space is full to capacity.

Evidence needed to evaluate the argument:

a) The percentage of Buckingham College students that live in dorms compared to the percentage who live in apartments.

b) The cost of room and board at Buckingham College compared to the cost of living in an apartment.

c) The rate of growth at the college over the past several years.

d) The reasons that students attend Buckingham College

e) Occupancy rate in the college dorms.

f) National trends regarding college attendance.

g) National population growth.

h) Demographics of students enrolled at Buckingham. Are they older students? Married students?

After completing these steps, you should have enough material to write your analysis. Remember that you are not creating a position of your own; you are evaluating the strengths and weaknesses of the existing argument. You do not have to include all of the points that you have created in your prewriting. In fact, during the process of drafting your analysis, other ideas may come to mind, and, if they strengthen your analysis, you should include them.

Sample Essay

The director of student housing is recommending the addition of considerable dormitory space at Buckingham College based on what appears to be continuing growth in enrollment at the college. More detailed information would help the college administrators make an informed decision. They should not rush into an expensive expansion without further research. Evaluating past and current trends, projected population growth, availability of off-campus housing, and the cost/benefit of constructing new dormitories among other concerns will assist them in analyzing the current and future condition of campus housing.

An important piece of evidence missing from the recommendation is the current occupancy rate of the existing dormitories. The housing director has not revealed whether or not the rooms are fully occupied or if some double rooms have had to be converted to triples. Has the college had to refuse dormitory space to some students desiring it? In fact, the housing director's final reason for building new dorms suggests that the college lacks students rather than dorm space. His or her prediction is that attractive dorms will attract more students to the college. One is left to wonder whether the school needs more dormitory space or more students.

Does evidence exist showing that students select a college based on the attractiveness of its dormitories? One need only look at some of the oldest colleges and universities in the United States to question the veracity of that reason for building new dorms. Selective schools like Harvard, Yale and Wellesley do not attract the top students from around the world because they provide luxurious living conditions. Students compete for a place at these schools because they will get the best education in the world, enabling them to become successful enough to build their own luxury homes. It would probably take relatively little time and effort to find survey results listing the top ten reasons given by students for choosing a particular college or university.

Another reason given by the director for building new dorms is the apparently rising cost of apartments in the town. The director does not provide specific figures comparing the cost of room and board on campus to the cost of rent, food and utilities associated with off-campus living. Students are apt to have more options for living off-campus. The housing director doesn't cite a shortage of apartments as a reason for building new dorms, so one may believe that students have a variety of apartment sizes and rents from which to choose. Students can split the cost of off-campus living with one or more roommates, an option not available in college dorms where the cost for each resident is the same.

Before investing in new dormitories, decision makers should see information about the types of students who attend Buckingham College. A considerable portion of the student body may be non-traditional students. They are older or married or attend only part time. They could be commuters who live at home and travel to campus only to attend classes. These students will not live in dorms. On the other hand, a campus populated with traditional students generally requires more dormitory space.

Competition for students to fill classrooms and dormitories has increased. Today, anyone can earn a college degree at any level without ever leaving home. The University of Phoenix, for example, offers bachelor's through doctorate degrees in a variety of disciplines. Students can log on to their classes at a time convenient for them, participate in discussions with other students from around the country, complete assignments, take exams, and see their grades while still in their pajamas. Even traditional colleges offer online versions of courses for degree credit. If this trend continues, neither Buckingham College nor other institutions of higher learning will need to increase dorm space.

Undertaking a capital expense like new dormitories is never done lightly. The decision to do so should not be based on the assumptions in the housing director's recommendation without further research. If those assumptions prove to be too optimistic, the college will need to find other ways to attract new students and accommodate the ones it already has.

Argument Task 19

The following appeared in the summary of a study on headaches suffered by the residents of Mentia.

"Salicylates are members of the same chemical family as aspirin, a medicine used to treat headaches. Although many foods are naturally rich in salicylates, for the past several decades, food-processing companies have also been adding salicylates to foods as preservatives. This rise in the commercial use of salicylates has been found to correlate with a steady decline in the average number of headaches reported by participants in our twenty-year study. Recently, food-processing companies have found that salicylates can also be used as flavor additives for foods. With this new use for salicylates, we can expect a continued steady decline in the number of headaches suffered by the average citizen of Mentia."

Write a response in which you discuss what specific evidence is needed to evaluate the argument and explain how the evidence would weaken or strengthen the argument.

Strategies

Argument:

Salicylates as flavor enhancers as well as preservatives will have an even greater ability to reduce the incidence of headaches in Mentia.

Facts and Assumptions:

a) Salicylates are members of the same chemical family as aspirin. The assumption is that they would act in the same manner as aspirin, that Salicylates are pain relievers.

b) Many foods are rich in Salicylates. One might assume that eating a diet comprised of those foods would help to prevent pain.

c) Food processing companies have been adding Salicylates to food as preservatives for several decades.

d) There has been a steady decline in the number of headaches reported by participants in a twenty-year study. The fact that this is a long-term study lends credence to any results reported out of it. The assumption is that the food additive has had a palliative effect on headaches.

e) The rise in the commercial use of Salicylates correlates with a reduction in headaches reported by participants in the study. This is an example of cause and effect.

f) Food companies have discovered that Salicylates can be used as flavor additives for foods. The assumption is that the companies will begin using Salicylates in this manner and that headaches will decline in greater numbers. An additional assumption is that people will buy these foods, perhaps in response to their greater curative powers.

Your notes do not have to be exhaustive. As you begin to write your essay, your brain will generate new ideas. Make certain that you keep the directions in mind as you develop your ideas.

Sample Essay

Although the results of the study suggest a direct link between the addition of Salicylates as a food preservative and a reduction in the reported number of headaches by participants in a study, blanks remain to be filled. Headaches can be annoying for some but debilitating for others. Treating headaches medically is a multi-million dollar industry. Treating headaches with a product that people are going to buy and consume as a matter of course would save individuals considerable amounts of money. The strength of the argument relies on evidence to support it.

The author of the study cited here purports that a reduction in headaches is linked to the addition of Salicylates as a preservative in processed foods. The reader needs evidence that the participants in the study actually ate a large amount of those foods on a regular basis. A question that arises concerns other treatments for headaches. Did the study participants use any analgesics to treat the headaches? Did they eat foods naturally high in Salicylates in addition to the processed foods? The participants may have sought alternative treatment such as acupuncture to relieve their headaches.

Will there be a further decline in the number of headaches when food processing companies use additional Salicylates in their products? It may be that the effectiveness of Salicylates has reached a saturation point. Compare this to the effectiveness of the humble aspirin. If two aspirin relieves a headache, would three be more palliative? What about side effects? Does the consumption of Salicylates in processed food cause some of the same complications as aspirin does? Some people are discouraged from taking aspirin because of its blood-thinning properties. Should the same caution be attached to Salicylates?

How does the addition of Salicylates affect the cost of processed food? Will adding even more, further raise prices? If that is the case, consumers may be reluctant to buy the products. Another factor to consider is the current move to natural and organic foods. Headache sufferers may decide that foods grown and processed without additional chemicals may have beneficial health effects.

At the very least, the reader needs more details about the lifestyles of the study participants to determine if Salicylates in processed food are the real heroes in this scenario. When all is revealed, the prediction about a further decline in headaches may not hold water.

Argument Task 20

The following appeared as part of a business plan developed by the manager of the Rialto Movie Theater.

"Despite its downtown location, the Rialto Movie Theater, a local institution for five decades, must make big changes or close its doors forever. It should follow the example of the new Apex Theater in the mall outside of town. When the Apex opened last year, it featured a video arcade, plush carpeting and seats, and a state-of-the-art sound system. Furthermore, in a recent survey, over 85 percent of respondents reported that the high price of newly released movies prevents them from going to the movies more than five times per year. Thus, if the Rialto intends to hold on to its share of a decreasing pool of moviegoers, it must offer the same features as Apex."

Write a response in which you discuss what questions would need to be answered in order to decide whether the recommendation is likely to have the predicted result. Be sure to explain how the answers to these questions would help to evaluate the recommendation.

Strategies

A good place to start your analysis is by creating a statement that reveals the main idea of the argument. Although the writer is creating an argument, he may ultimately be stating a position, making a recommendation, or making a prediction. It may be helpful for you to determine which of these formats is most evident in the argument.

In an effort to increase profits and prevent the closing of the Rialto Theater, the manager recommends that the business take the same steps that the Apex took when it opened last year.

Assumptions:

a) What works in a mall location will work in a downtown location.

b) The Apex Theater is profitable.

c) People went to movies more frequently when the prices were lower.

d) Fewer people go to the movies now than in the past.

e) The downtown location has always contributed to the Rialto's success.

Questions:

a) Who responded to the survey, and how large was the sample?

b) How profitable is the Apex?

c) What types of movies are shown at each theater?

d) Has attendance at the Rialto declined?

e) What other factors may be contributing to the Rialto's predicted closing?

f) Has the parking situation changed in the downtown area?

g) Have businesses that used to attract people to the downtown closed or moved to the mall?

After completing these steps, you should have enough material to write your analysis. Remember that you are not creating a position of your own; you are evaluating the strengths and weaknesses of the existing argument. You do not have to include all of the points that you have created in your prewriting. In fact, during the process of drafting your analysis, other ideas may come to mind, and, if they strengthen your analysis, you should include them.

Sample Essay

A good business plan depends on sufficient detailed information. Its creator must have answers to a number of questions to prove the reliability of the plan. The purpose of a business plan is generally to obtain funding, in this case to make significant changes to the Rialto Movie Theater. Before a bank or other investors open their checkbooks, the manager must answer questions about the Rialto's situation rather than provide general information about the competition.

The manager cites a survey about the cost of attending new releases and how it discourages movie goers from seeing more than five of them per year. Before making expensive changes based on this survey, the manager should ask who responded to the survey. The sample may be limited to a specific age group, for example. If the respondents were young families or senior citizens, they would have less discretionary income than some other age groups. Regardless of who completed the survey, if money prevents them from attending, adding attractions or improving the interior of the theater won't make them attend the movies more frequently. In fact, movie attendees' spending money on other attractions at the theater like a video arcade may reduce the amount that they can spend to actually purchase tickets to the show. It's always important to know who requested the survey and for what purpose. Missing from the survey is information about the types of movies the respondents prefer, what times of the year and days of the week they choose to attend movies. That information could help the Rialto tailor its movie selection and on which days to open and the number of times to show a film each day.

This business plan does not mention attendance numbers. Has attendance at the Rialto declined, or have other events led to the dire prediction of the theater's closing? Other than a decline in attendance, a rise in expenses can contribute to lower profits. Steady attendance at traditional prices means little if other costs of operation have increased. The cost of heating and/or cooling may be higher than last year. The same number of ticket buyers at the same prices as last year cannot support any unexpected expenses.

It appears that the downtown location has served the Rialto well for several decades. Has the downtown undergone some changes? Unfortunately, downtowns across the country have faced many challenges from mall development and big box stores. Independently-owned small businesses have been forced to close or move to the malls where traffic is heavier. Without business to drive citizens to the downtown, the Rialto may be unable to attract crowds large enough to make it profitable. Another possibility is that a large business of some type, a call center, for example, may have filled the empty buildings in the downtown. Operating 24 hours a day, the center's employees may be using parking lots or spaces that movie goers previously used. Without sufficient parking, the Rialto cannot hope to fill its seats.

Although the argument reveals the added attractions at the Apex, it does not reveal whether or not the Apex is profitable. Despite the video arcade, plush seats and state-of-the-art sound system, the Apex's expenses may make it unprofitable. It would be helpful to know if the video arcade contributes to the bottom line in a significant way or if people's patronizing the arcade has a negative effect on theater attendance.

Making big changes will require the Rialto to spend big bucks. Before going to that extreme, the Rialto must analyze all the results of the survey and how conditions in the downtown have changed in recent years. If there are insurmountable obstacles, the manager's recommendation may prove fruitless.

Argument Task 21

The following appeared on the Mozart School of Music Web site.

"The Mozart School of Music should be the first choice for parents considering enrolling their child in music lessons. First of all, the Mozart School welcomes youngsters at all ability and age levels; there is no audition to attend the school. Second, the school offers instruction in nearly all musical instruments as well a wide range of styles and genres from classical to rock. Third, the faculty includes some of the most distinguished musicians in the area. Finally, many Mozart graduates have gone on to become well-known and highly paid professional musicians."

Write a response in which you examine the stated and/or unstated assumptions of the argument. Be sure to explain how the argument depends on these assumptions and what the implications are for the argument if the assumptions prove unwarranted.

Strategies

A good place to start your analysis is by creating a statement that reveals the main idea of the argument. Although the writer is creating an argument, he may ultimately be stating a position, making a recommendation, or making a prediction. It may be helpful for you to determine which of these formats is most evident in the argument.

The author of this website uses several claims about the Mozart School of Music to support the recommendation that parents choose the school for their children's music education.

Assumptions:

a) Mozart School of Music is the best place for anyone who wants to learn to play a musical instrument.

b) Students who attend Mozart are more likely to become successful musicians.

c) Distinguished musicians are effective teachers.

d) Other schools require an audition as part of the application process.

e) Auditions are undesirable.

f) Distinguished musicians teach at all ability levels.

g) Mozart School of Music is affordable.

h) The school has convenient hours of operation.

i) All who apply will be accepted.

Alternative explanations:

a) Mozart may be the only music school.

b) Distinguished musicians are ineffective teachers.

c) Distinguished musicians teach only advanced students.

After completing these steps, you should have enough material to write your analysis. Remember that you are not creating a position of your own; you are evaluating the strengths and weaknesses of the existing argument. You do not have to include all of the points that you have created in your prewriting. In fact, during the process of drafting your analysis, other ideas may come to mind, and, if they strengthen your analysis, you should include them.

Sample Essay

Of course, the owner of a business website is not going to include information that would discourage viewers from buying its product or service. The Mozart School of Music is no exception. In an effort to boost enrollment, the school cites some appealing facts that should lead those seeking music lessons for their children to assume Mozart School of Music can meet all of their needs. Visitors to the site may rely on incorrect assumptions when choosing the Mozart School of Music.

Based on the claims listed, parents may assume that their child will be in a class or lesson taught by a local, distinguished musician. The fact of the matter may be that distinguished musicians make up a small percentage of the total teaching staff, or they teach only advanced students. Those distinguished musicians may all be piano teachers, so anyone seeking to play the flute, saxophone, drums, etc. will not have one of these musicians as an instructor. These musicians may also be restricted to one style of music. If they are all jazz aficionados, children seeking to learn classical music will be in classes taught by less distinguished musicians. There is no guarantee that these musicians are effective instructors. They may have little patience for the stumbling, tentative attempts at music that young children are likely to display. Parents and/or students may demand to be placed with one of those distinguished musicians and go elsewhere if their demands aren't met. The website fails to reveal the qualifications of its instructors who are not distinguished musicians. Potential students need to know what kind of education and experience all of Mozart's instructors have.

No mention is made on the website about hours of operation, convenience of location, or cost of lessons. Since children are in school all day, and most parents work, those seeking lessons may assume that the Mozart School of Music will accommodate families by offering lessons after school, in the evenings, and on weekends. Location is important. If the school is located in an out-of-the-way place or in an area that lacks parking, many potential students may not be able to get there. Parents may assume that the lessons are reasonably priced, or they may conclude, based on the information, that the lessons are too pricey. Parents should also ask if lessons with one of the distinguished musicians on staff cost more than lessons with other instructors. One might also ask if the school provides instruments, either for rent or sale and their cost. Lesson materials are another expense that prospective students will need to consider.

Parents may assume that all who apply to the Mozart School of Music will be accepted, since auditions are not required. This assumption may be unrealistic as the school is not likely to have unlimited space. It is also difficult to imagine how they place students in a class or individual lessons without an audition to determine their level of accomplishment. Parents and their children may be leery of a school that does not allow them to show what they know before being placed with an instructor. It smacks of desperation that the school accepts everyone who applies or can pay. Visitors to the website may assume that the school is neither very successful nor discriminating.

Mozart School of Music's claim of superiority may lead visitors to the site to assume that there are several other schools that are inferior. Mozart, in fact, may be the only school. Conversely, it may be facing stiff competition from several other music schools, compelling its directors to make it sound attractive and emphasize the ease with which students are accepted. The fact that many of Mozart's graduates have gone on to become highly-paid professionals may actually deter some students from choosing this school. They may assume that the school applies pressure for its students to excel. This could intimidate students who want to learn to play an instrument for personal pleasure.

Parents of children who want music lessons should carefully examine the assumptions they might make after visiting Mozart School of Music's website. Without sufficient evidence, they could enroll their children in a school where distinguished musicians do little besides instruct the most superior students and whose cost and hours of operation make it an inconvenient choice.

Argument Task 22

The following appeared in an editorial in a local newspaper.

"Commuters complain that increased rush-hour traffic on Blue Highway between the suburbs and the city center has doubled their commuting time. The favored proposal of the motorists' lobby is to widen the highway, adding an additional lane of traffic. Opponents note that last year's addition of a lane to the nearby Green Highway was followed by a worsening of traffic jams on it. Their suggested alternative proposal is adding a bicycle lane to Blue Highway. Many area residents are keen bicyclists. A bicycle lane would encourage them to use bicycles to commute, it is argued, thereby reducing rush-hour traffic."

Write a response in which you discuss what questions would need to be answered in order to decide whether the recommendation and the argument on which it is based are reasonable. Be sure to explain how the answers to these questions would help to evaluate the recommendation.

Strategies

Argument:

The city should add a bike lane to Blue Highway to reduce congestion on the highway during rush hours.

In developing your response, you are asked to discuss what questions need to be answered before the city takes this step and how the answers to those questions will affect the decision.

Facts and Assumptions:

a) Commuters are complaining that traffic during rush hour on Blue Highway has doubled their commuting time between the suburbs and the city center. The assumption is that the highway doesn't have sufficient room for all of the commuters.

b) The motorists' lobby wants to widen the highway by adding another lane. They assume that an additional lane will lessen commuting time by providing more space for the cars on the highway.

c) Worsening traffic jams followed the addition of a lane to Green Highway last year. The assumption is that an additional lane is not the answer to commuter problems.

d) Many area residents are keen bicyclists. The writer assumes that many of them would like to ride their bikes to work.

Questions:

a) How much of an increase in traffic is there? Why has commuting time doubled?

b) Is Green Highway still experiencing traffic jams? Was it a temporary situation?

c) Who are the opponents to the proposed extra lane? Are they homeowners who may be displaced by the expansion or whose homes will be too close to the road when it is expanded? Are they developers who have other ideas for using the land over which the new lane will travel?

d) Who are the keen bicyclists? Are they children or adults?

e) How practical is a bike lane for commuters? Are bikers willing to travel in the dark during the winter months? Does the area experience cold, snowy winters? Will commuters travel by bike in the rain? Will traveling by bike take more time each way?

Your notes do not have to be exhaustive. As you begin to write your essay, your brain will generate new ideas. Make certain that you keep the directions in mind as you develop your ideas.

Sample Essay

An editorial is usually written by an editor and expresses the position of the newspaper on a particular topic. The excerpt provided here simply presents both sides of an issue. On one side are motorists who are frustrated by the increased traffic and commuter travel time on Blue Highway and think that an additional lane would relieve the problem. On the opposing side are those who point to problems on Green Highway since the addition of a lane there and think that the addition of a bike lane is the answer. A number of questions need answers before planners take either action.

The reader knows that motorists are in favor of an additional highway lane. Who are the opponents? Several groups come to mind. Homeowners who live near the highway may fear being displaced or encroached upon by a highway expansion. They may be worried about the increased noise. It could lower property values, and the homeowners could face challenges when trying to sell their houses. Commercial developers may have their sights set on the land that would be needed for a highway expansion. The possibility of new jobs and a broader tax base may trump commuter comfort.

Is a bike lane a viable option? It may be if this highway is in a part of the country where the daylight hours are always long, and the sun always shines. If the highway is in a location where the days are shorter in the winter months, workers may jump in their cars to travel safely in the dark. When it rains or snows or gets cold, commuters are likely to opt for their cars in favor of bikes. If one of the aims is to reduce commuting time, a bike route may not be the answer. Bikes do not travel at the same speeds as cars.

Is Green Highway still experiencing traffic jams? Was the additional lane the cause of traffic jams, or was traffic diverted to the newly expanded Green Highway as a result of road construction elsewhere? It may have been a temporary situation .Because it happened on Green Highway is no guarantee that traffic will snarl on Blue Highway. All of these questions deserve consideration before any final decisions are made regarding any type of expansion of Blue Highway.

Argument Task 23

Since those issues of Newsbeat magazine that featured political news on their front cover were the poorest-selling issues over the past three years, the publisher of Newsbeat has recommended that the magazine curtail its emphasis on politics to focus more exclusively on economics and personal finance. She points to a recent survey of readers of general interest magazines that indicate greater reader interest in economic issues than in political ones. Newsbeat's editor, however, opposes the proposed shift in editorial policy, pointing out that very few magazines offer extensive political coverage anymore.

Write a response in which you discuss what questions would need to be answered in order to decide whether the recommendation and the argument on which it is based are reasonable. Be sure to explain how the answers to these questions would help to evaluate the recommendation.

Strategies

A good place to start your analysis is by creating a statement that reveals the main idea of the argument. Although the writer is creating an argument, he may ultimately be stating a position, making a recommendation, or making a prediction. It may be helpful for you to determine which of these formats is most evident in the argument.

In order to revive sales of Newsbeat, the publisher, against the advice of the editor, suggests shifting the magazines' focus from politics to economics and personal finance.

Assumptions:

a) Political news on the cover rather than other content is responsible for decreased sales of certain issues of the magazine.

b) Readers of general interest magazines will begin to read Newsbeat if the magazine changes its focus.

c) Sales of Newsbeat magazine will rise if it features more stories about economics and personal finance.

d) There is room in the marketplace for another magazine with a focus on economics and personal finance.

e) Sales of magazines that feature articles on economics and personal finance are higher than sales of Newsbeat.

Questions that need answers in order to decide whether the recommendation and argument are reasonable:

a) What other factors may have contributed to lower sales of those issues?

b) Were those poorest-selling issues published in the same year, or were they evenly distributed over the three-year period?

c) Has the magazine surveyed its own readers to learn their preferences?

d) How many issues features political news on their covers?

e) Were any of those years election years?

f) Does Newsbeat have staff writers capable of writing about economics and personal finance?

g) Is there a market for another magazine that focuses on economics and personal finance?

h) Have magazines that feature articles about economics and personal finance continued to sell well?

i) Why is there an apparently strong interest in information about economics and personal finance?

After completing these steps, you should have enough material to write your analysis. Remember that you are not creating a position of your own; you are evaluating the strengths and weaknesses of the existing argument. You do not have to include all of the points that you have created in your prewriting. In fact, during the process of drafting your analysis, other ideas may come to mind, and, if they strengthen your analysis, you should include them.

Sample Essay

The publisher of Newsbeat magazine should not be too hasty to change the format of the publication. Using a survey of readers of general interest magazines to determine the future course of Newsbeat is akin to comparing apples to oranges. Before making costly changes, this publisher should ask several important questions that will help her determine the editorial decisions she should make to improve Newsbeat's circulation.

Did the three-year dip in sales occur in the period between national elections? It's logical to expect that interest in political news would peak during election years and wane in the other three years. The publisher does not reveal whether or not this three-year dip is typical throughout the magazine's history. If that is, indeed, the case, the publisher and editor should make decisions about some changes in focus during the dips and continue to focus on politics during the fourth year. The focus on politics may not be the real reason for the dip in sales. Are the articles poorly written, or do they express unpopular opinions? They may not be objective enough, offending half of the potential readers. The articles may not be timely, or they may be too regional in nature.

Has Newsbeat conducted its own survey of readers? If Newsbeat wants information about the preferences of its reader, the magazine should conduct its own survey. The questions on the survey cited in the argument may have been worded to elicit specific answers. Using survey results out of context can be misleading. Just because readers of general interest magazines prefer articles about economics and personal finance to articles about politics may not indicate that the same is true for readers of Newsbeat. In fact, the respondents may prefer articles about fashion or entertainment above all others, and articles about economics may be very near the bottom of their list of favorites. They may not buy Newsbeat whatever its focus.

Focusing on economics and personal finance may increase Newsbeat's circulation, but that may be short-lived if the articles are poorly written. Does Newsbeat have writers on its staff who are capable of writing in depth about those topics? If Newsbeat is forced to hire writers whose expertise is in the field of finance, the expense may not be offset by increased sales. Alternatively, the publisher may be forced to lay off seasoned political writers to hire finance writers, and, when she needs them during election years, they will not be available. This strategy could result in a death spiral for Newsbeat.

Looking at the periodicals section of a grocery store or book store reveals the wide variety of genres available. There's something for everyone. As a corollary, there must be someone for everything. There must be an audience for a news magazine. The method used by that audience to gain access to magazines has changed. Has Newsbeat tried another format to attract readers? Like so many other publications, Newsbeat may have to create an online presence. They may have to use some form of social media to increase exposure to the magazine. If Newsbeat has not made subscriptions available in the past, perhaps they should do so now.

Are poor sales of issues with political topics featured on the cover a cause for great concern? If the magazine is published every month, 36 issues would have appeared in a three-year span. If one or two per year featured political stories, the lower sales of those particular issues should not be the only reason to change the magazine's focus. For any issue to have the poorest sales in any given year, the sales total only has to be one dollar less than the next- lowest-selling issue. The publisher may be overstating her case for change.

Based on current trends in periodicals and the manner in which people gain access to information of any kind, not only Newsbeat, but every magazine may be in peril. Any change that the publisher and editor can agree on should be taken with caution. Depending on the answers to important questions, they may be saving this magazine, and they may be throwing good money after bad in an effort to increase circulation.

Argument Task 24

In a study of the reading habits of Waymarsh citizens conducted by the University of Waymarsh, most respondents said they preferred literary classics as reading material. However, a second study conducted by the same researchers found that the type of book most frequently checked out of each of the public libraries in Waymarsh was the mystery novel. Therefore, it can be concluded that the respondents in the first study had misrepresented their reading preferences.

Write a response in which you examine the stated and/or unstated assumptions of the argument. Be sure to explain how the argument depends on these assumptions and what the implications are for the argument if the assumptions prove unwarranted.

Strategies

A good place to start your analysis is by creating a statement that reveals the main idea of the argument. Although the writer is creating an argument, he may ultimately be stating a position, making a recommendation, or making a prediction. It may be helpful for you to determine which of these formats is most evident in the argument.

It is the author's contention that the citizens of Waymarsh misrepresented their reading preferences on two surveys conducted by the University of Waymarsh.

Assumptions:

a) Survey respondents got their literary classics from the library.

b) Respondents lied on the survey.

c) The survey sample was large.

d) Respondents to both surveys were the same.

e) Both surveys measured the same thing.

f) The surveys were conducted in a short period of time.

g) The survey was unbiased.

Alternative explanations:

a) Respondents were different for each survey.

b) Those who prefer to read the classics own the books.

c) Respondents to the second survey misrepresented their choices.

d) The surveys were conducted in different years.

e) The surveys served different purposes.

f) The survey samples were small.

g) The libraries have more mystery novels available than classics.

h) The libraries do not have classics on their shelves.

i) The term, classic, was not clearly defined on the survey.

j) Classics were checked out of the university's library.

k) Respondents read the classics in the reading rooms at the public libraries.

After completing these steps, you should have enough material to write your analysis. Remember that you are not creating a position of your own; you are evaluating the strengths and weaknesses of the existing argument. You do not have to include all of the points that you have created in your prewriting. In fact, during the process of drafting your analysis, other ideas may come to mind, and, if they strengthen your analysis, you should include them.

Sample Essay

The power of the survey must be used judicially. Without knowing what a survey is designed to measure, the results can be misinterpreted or manipulated. The surveys cited in this argument appear to reveal information about the reading habits of Waymarsh citizens, and, on the surface, appear to contradict each other. Closer analysis of the assumptions that led to the conclusion in the argument may bring alternative explanations to light.

The reader may assume that the surveys were conducted over a short period of time. However, given enough time between the two, it would be reasonable to expect that reading habits have changed. Even though the same group conducted the survey, they may have done the two projects four years apart. The respondents may have been the same, but, in a four-year span, they may have read all of the classics they wanted to and moved on to mystery novels.

The survey may not have provided a clear definition of the term, classic. Assuming that everyone has the same understanding of that term may have led to some faulty responses to the questions. Respondents to the survey may have had various understandings of the classic. The Maltese Falcon, for example, is often described as a classic detective novel; The Great Gatsby is a classic portrayal of the Roaring Twenties; The Grapes of Wrath is a classic depiction of the dispossessed. The creators of the survey may have had novels from the nineteenth century in mind. There is too little information in the argument to determine their intentions. On the other hand, it may have been clear to the respondents what constitutes a classic. The libraries in Waymarsh may have a limited number of classics on their shelves, so even those who prefer reading classics check out other types of novels when a classic that they have not read is unavailable.

Surveys must be free of bias to obtain accurate results. The wording of each question on the survey must avoid leading the respondents to select one answer over another. Qualifiers like better or worse can cause a respondent to select an answer that he thinks will please the creators of a survey. This invalidates the results.

Even though the same group conducted both surveys, assuming that each was designed for the same purpose, creates an unsustainable conclusion. The first survey may have been designed to determine the reading preferences of the respondents. It appears to have done that. The second survey may have sought to determine what genres are most frequently checked out of the local libraries. If so, it accomplished that goal. To presume that the respondents to the first survey misled the researchers fails if the surveys did not have the same goal.

The second survey discovered that mysteries were checked out of the public libraries more frequently than books of other genres. The readers of the survey may assume that respondents to the survey only use public libraries to obtain reading material. The argument does not mention if there are other libraries in Waymarsh. Churches frequently have libraries. The city may have a literary society that provides copies of the classics to its patrons. The university itself must have a library. Any of these may provide copies of classics to the readers in Waymarsh. In fact, the readers of classics may not borrow the books from any source. They may choose to relax in the reading rooms of the various libraries. The public libraries may have the classics on CDs which borrowers may check out and listen to in their homes or cars.

Overall, too little information is present in the argument to support the conclusion reached by the researchers from Waymarsh University. It does not even reveal if the surveys were written or administered orally. One might assume that the researchers are from the English department from the university and use the information in the surveys to inform their curriculum or instruction. However, the researchers may be from the psychology or sociology department of the university, and they conduct the surveys to measure emotional responses to the questions. The argument cannot stand because of the missing information.

Argument Task 25

The following appeared in a memorandum written by the vice president of Health Naturally, a small but expanding chain of stores selling health food and other health-related products.

"Our previous experience has been that our stores are most profitable in areas where residents are highly concerned with leading healthy lives. We should therefore build one of our new stores in Plainsville, which clearly has many such residents. Plainsville merchants report that sales of running shoes and exercise equipment are at all-time highs. The local health club, which nearly closed five years ago due to lack of business, has more members than ever and the weight-training and aerobics classes are always full. We can even anticipate a new generation of customers: Plainsville's schoolchildren are required to participate in a program called Fitness for Life, which emphasizes the benefits of regular exercise at an early age."

Write a response in which you discuss what specific evidence is needed to evaluate the argument and explain how the evidence would weaken or strengthen the argument.

Strategies

A good place to start your analysis is by creating a statement that reveals the main idea of the argument. Although the writer is creating an argument, he may ultimately be stating a position, making a recommendation, or making a prediction. It may be helpful for you to determine which of these formats is most evident in the argument.

Based on reports from local merchants and health club owner, the vice president of Health Naturally proposes building one of their new stores in Plainsville.

Assumptions:

a) Plainsville citizens will continue to attend the health club in the same numbers in the future.

b) The health club has always offered weight-training and aerobics classes.

c) The current population of school children will remain in Plainsville

d) The health club has substantially greater membership than it did five years ago.

e) There are no stores in Plainsville that sell health foods and other health-related items.

f) Plainsville has a population large enough to support a Health Naturally store.

g) People who exercise buy health foods.

Alternative explanations:

a) The increase in numbers occurred at the beginning of the year- New Year's resolutions

b) The health club may have upgraded its equipment and added new classes.

c) Competing health clubs may have closed.

d) The health club is open during more convenient hours.

e) Residents are able to buy health foods at the local grocery store.

f) The all-time high in sales of running shoes and other exercise equipment is a very small increase over the second-best year.

After completing these steps, you should have enough material to write your analysis. Remember that you are not creating a position of your own; you are evaluating the strengths and weaknesses of the existing argument. You do not have to include all of the points that you have created in your prewriting. In fact, during the process of drafting your analysis, other ideas may come to mind, and, if they strengthen your analysis, you should include them.

Sample Essay

Health Naturally is expanding, and, like any well-run company, has researched existing conditions before deciding which towns to select for its new stores. Using past experience, Health Naturally has determined that Plainsville is a suitable location. The company vice president has loaded his memo with highly charged words in an effort to persuade others to adopt his recommendation. "All-time high", "more than ever", and "always full" make the future in Plainsville sound very promising. These descriptors mean little or nothing when taken out of context.

When Plainsville merchants claim that sales of running shoes are at an all-time high, they don't reveal by how much in dollars or how many units sold. Sales in total dollars would just have to be one dollar higher than the previous best year to be considered an all-time high. The high dollar amount might be a result of an increase in the prices of running shoes. The merchants may actually have sold fewer pairs of shoes. The number of units sold might be a better measure of greater-than-ever success, but, again, selling one more pair of shoes than in the previous best year should not determine the health consciousness of Plainsville residents. If the conditions stated here are true, they do not support the argument put forth by Health Naturally's vice president.

The health club in Plainsville also appears to be thriving, claiming more members than ever before. A total membership of one more than the previous best year supports this claim, but one additional member is not sufficient to justify the expense of building a Health Naturally store in this location. In fact, this company should seek to know why the health club had so little business five years ago. There may have been several other clubs in the area that actually have closed in the intervening years, leaving this club as the only one still standing. When members of the closed clubs sought another place to exercise, they had no other choice but the club in Plainsville. This same situation explains why the aerobics and weight-training classes are always full. On the other hand, the health club may have reduced the number of classes, causing those who want to attend to crowd in to those available. Membership in the health club may fluctuate throughout the year. Some of the most popular New Year's resolutions are to lose weight and to adopt a healthier life style. If Health Naturally interviewed the merchants and the health club owner shortly after the beginning of the New Year, their numbers may be inflated. If those interviews took place in May or September, for example, the numbers reported could be a reason for optimism.

A presumption in this argument is that people who exercise will buy health foods, and they will buy them at a Health Naturally store. If the residents of Plainsville buy natural foods, they must already have a source for it, maybe even the local grocery store. Getting people to change their shopping habits is expensive and time consuming and, ultimately, may not be possible. Knowing the socioeconomic status of Plainsville residents would help Health Naturally make a decision about locating there. Natural foods are generally more expensive than foods carried in typical grocery stores.

If the income levels in Plainsville are too low, the new health store will probably fail.

Finally, the vice president of the company assumes that the children of Plainsville are sure to become future customers of the store. Because the children must participate in a Fitness for Life program, they will continue to practice what they learn. A piece of information that would help determine the veracity of this assumption is the employment picture in Plainsville. Unless today's children can be assured of employment as adults, they will have to leave to seek their fortunes elsewhere.

The vice president of Health Naturally needs more detailed evidence to support his proposal to establish one of the company's new stores in Plainsville. It may turn out that this town is indeed health conscious and would welcome a store offering products that enhances their lifestyle choice. In contrast, further evidence may reveal the shallow nature of the apparent healthy behavior in Plainsville, and the decision to locate a new store in another location would be the wisest one.

Argument Task 26

The following appeared in a memorandum from the manager of WWAC radio station.

"WWAC must change from its current rock-music format because the number of listeners has been declining, even though the population in our listening area has been growing. The population growth has resulted mainly from people moving to our area after their retirement, and we must make listeners of these new residents. But they seem to have limited interest in music: several local stores selling recorded music have recently closed. Therefore, just changing to another kind of music is not going to increase our audience. Instead, we should adopt a news-and-talk format, a form of radio that is increasingly popular in our area."

Write a response in which you discuss what questions would need to be answered in order to decide whether the recommendation and the argument on which it is based are reasonable. Be sure to explain how the answers to these questions would help to evaluate the recommendation.

NOTE: The above topic has wording similar to Agrument Task 27 of GRE Analytical Writing Solutions to the Real Essay Topics - Book 1. However, if you read carefully you will notice that the task instructions are different. Hence, it is very important to read the topic as well as its instructions completely before you start to write your response.

Strategies

A good place to start your analysis is by creating a statement that reveals the main idea of the argument. Although the writer is creating an argument, he may ultimately be stating a position, making a recommendation, or making a prediction. It may be helpful for you to determine which of these formats is most evident in the argument.

WWAC's station manager has tied a reduction in its listeners to the closings of local music stores and associates that with a lack of interest in music in general, leading to his recommendation to change the format of the station to news and talk shows.

Assumptions:

a) The new residents have little interest in music.

b) Stores have closed because the new residents have little interest in music.

c) Changing its format will allow WWAC to attract more listeners.

d) WWAC will be able to attract listeners from other news-and-talk format stations in the area.

e) People in the area no longer listen to rock music.

f) Retirees prefer news and talk shows.

Questions:

a) Has WWAC made changes in its hours of operation that might account for a decline in listeners?

b) Has another radio station gone on-air in the area, providing competition for WWAC?

c) How much more popular is the talk-show format than it used to be?

d) Do the rock music shows air when they can attract large audiences?

e) Are news-and-talk shows popular with retirees?

f) Has WWAC hired new on-air talent?

After completing these steps, you should have enough material to write your analysis. Remember that you are not creating a position of your own; you are evaluating the strengths and weaknesses of the existing argument. You do not have to include all of the points that you have created in your prewriting. In fact, during the process of drafting your analysis, other ideas may come to mind, and, if they strengthen your analysis, you should include them.

Sample Essay

News and talk shows have become pervasive on the radio and television airways over the past few decades. At virtually any time of day, one can tune in to a talk show either on radio or television. The number of stations focusing exclusively on news in each medium has also exploded. The advent of cable television, the Internet, and satellite radio puts news and talk at everybody's fingertips 24/7/365. The assumption that switching to this format based on the brief and vague information in the argument needs further verification before taking this drastic action.

Tying the closing of music stores to the apparent lack of interest in music may be a faulty assumption. Other explanations might be as valid. The proliferation of music competition shows on television and the longevity of these programs demonstrates a continued interest in music by people of all ages. If viewing audiences decline, advertisers may pull their sponsorship of these shows, and they will be off the air in short order. People are listening to music in different ways today. No longer does a jazz aficionado place an lp on a turntable; he downloads his favorite tunes from iTunes onto his iPod nano, plugs in his ear buds, and goes out for a run. Music of all genres is more accessible than it has ever been. If people didn't buy it, record companies would not produce it. Brick-and-mortar music stores have not fared well in the twenty first century but not as a result of declining interest in music.

Assuming that WWAC can make listeners of the retirees that have moved to the area by switching formats may be an exercise in futility. It is likely that many of them are living on fixed incomes and have little discretionary income to spend on entertainment. They might watch a lot of television and spend minimal time listening to the radio. This lack of spending money may contribute to the supposed lack of interest in music. They cannot afford to buy albums. On the other hand, they may have purchased all of the music they need before retiring. They either don't need or want to accumulate more possessions of any kind.

More people listen to the radio during drive time - the periods spent driving to and from work- than any other time of day. The assumption that retirees should be WWAC's target audience could eliminate a larger number of listeners. Perhaps, WWAC should focus their appeal to those who work every day. Those commuters may prefer music of any genre to news reports that can be disturbing or talk shows that can be strident.

Just as they develop shopping habits, people develop listening habits. Attracting customers or listeners is generally a time-consuming and expensive proposition. Because there are already radio stations that have a news and talk-show format in the area, WWAC may have to go the extra mile to become successful in that market. The assumption that attracting new listeners is more cost effective than trying to maintain the listeners they already have could lead to unnecessary spending. They must offer shows that are different from and better than those already being aired. They will need to convince their sponsors that they can increase the number of listeners. If WWAC plans to use syndicated shows, the station will have to pay fees to the owners of those shows. Those listeners who currently tune in to hear rock music could abandon the station for another that plays rock. WWAC will not only need to attract new listeners, it will have to replace those it loses as a result of the change in format.

WWAC needs to conduct some market research before relying on the assumptions in the argument and abandoning its current format. A more varied mix of genres may help. Those retirees may, indeed, listen to the radio, but they prefer jazz or standards. The station may need to change its hours of operation. The local market may be saturated with talk and news shows. Without more detailed information, WWAC may make a decision that will lead to its going off the air.

Argument Task 27

The following appeared in an e-mail sent by the marketing director of the Classical Shakespeare Theatre of Bardville.

"Over the past ten years, there has been a 20 percent decline in the size of the average audience at Classical Shakespeare Theatre productions. In spite of increased advertising, we are attracting fewer and fewer people to our shows, causing our profits to decrease significantly. We must take action to attract new audience members. The best way to do so is by instituting a 'Shakespeare in the Park' program this summer. Two years ago the nearby Avon Repertory Company started a 'Free Plays in the Park' program, and its profits have increased 10 percent since then. If we start a 'Shakespeare in the Park' program, we can predict that our profits will increase, too."

Write a response in which you discuss what questions would need to be answered in order to decide whether the recommendation is likely to have the predicted result. Be sure to explain how the answers to these questions would help to evaluate the recommendation.

Strategies

A good place to start your analysis is by creating a statement that reveals the main idea of the argument. Although the writer is creating an argument, he may ultimately be stating a position, making a recommendation, or making a prediction. It may be helpful for you to determine which of these formats is most evident in the argument.

The marketing director believes that imitating Avon Repertory Company's Free Plays in the Park program will increase attendance at Classical Shakespeare Theatre productions.

Assumptions:

a) Profits are tied to attendance.

b) The decline in attendance at Classical Shakespeare Theatre productions has occurred steadily over the past ten years.

c) They are advertising in locations and publications that have worked for them in the past.

d) Avon Repertory Company's profits have increased because of their Free Plays in the Park program.

Questions:

a) Has Classical Shakespeare Theatre changed its repertoire?

b) Should the company change its repertoire?

c) Has the company changed the type of advertising it does?

d) Has Avon Repertory Company taken other measures to increase profits?

e) Does one particular year account for most of the decline?

f) Do any particular plays draw larger audiences than others?

After completing these steps, you should have enough material to write your analysis. Remember that you are not creating a position of your own; you are evaluating the strengths and weaknesses of the existing argument. You do not have to include all of the points that you have created in your prewriting. In fact, during the process of drafting your analysis, other ideas may come to mind, and, if they strengthen your analysis, you should include them.

Sample Essay

Declining audience numbers is a legitimate concern for Classical Shakespeare Company. Efforts on the part of the company appear to have been ineffective, so they propose to duplicate the actions of Avon Repertory Company whose success appears to be on the rise. There is always danger associated with abandoning what one has always done. Change may be necessary, but the shape of that change must be carefully considered. One size does not always fit all. The marketing director needs answers to several questions before making the suggested changes.

An average is derived by adding a specific number of figures and dividing the total by that number. Some numbers are higher than the average, and some are lower. There may be a significant span between the highest and lowest numbers. Have some of Classical Shakespeare Theatre's productions had very poor attendance while others have standing-room-only attendance? This theater company may be able to solve attendance problems by discontinuing production of the plays that draw small audiences and increasing the number of performances of the plays that draw large audiences. The company may also benefit from changing the times of the performances. Are the largest reductions in attendance occurring consistently for performances on certain days of the work or specific times of the day? Changing days and times would be a relatively simple fix for the attendance problem. Avon Repertory Company may have been paying attention to these details and plays to full houses as a result.

Virtually all commercial enterprises use advertising to encourage the public to buy its product or use its service. Classical Shakespeare Company has used advertising in the past and has recently expanded its advertising in an effort to increase attendance at its productions. This tactic appears to have failed. Has the company changed the type of advertising it does or advertised in different publications? This theater company should research the reach of the advertising, perhaps by surveying their audience members. They may need to shift advertising dollars from print sources to radio or television. If the company has increased its television advertising, its ads may be appearing at times in the station's rotation when theater goers are not tuned in. If they are advertising upcoming productions that historically have had low attendance, they are likely to have wasted their money. The company may have changed advertising agencies, and the new agency has no experience creating ads for the entertainment industry.

Rather than look outside of the theater to improve attendance, Classical Shakespeare Company might look at the condition of the theater itself. Has the company taken steps to ensure that the audience enjoys attending performances at its theater? The seats may be worn and uncomfortable. The heating and cooling system may work inefficiently. If the audience finds it difficult to sit in the seats, or they are too cold or too warm, they may abandon this company for another that has renovated, making the theater experience more pleasurable. In fact, the condition of its theater may be the reason that Avon Repertory Company has increased profits rather than its Free Plays in the Park. Is the company's payroll too large? Employees are a big expense, and producing plays requires a variety of skilled workers in addition to the actors themselves. On- stage talent usually receive the biggest paychecks. This can be a double-edged sword. A theater company can hire better actors in an effort to draw bigger audiences, or it can hire lesser-known actors to reduce the overall payroll. If the payroll is smaller, the company's bottom line looks better. The risk is smaller audiences. Theater companies must strike a delicate balance when casting its productions.

A theater company experiencing financial uncertainty may only ensure its demise by taking on a project that has no proven benefit. Before imitating Avon Repertory Company's Free Plays in the Park, the Classical Shakespeare Company should ask if that program directly contributes to Avon's increase in profits. Classical Shakespeare Company should scrutinize its past and current practices and answer some tough questions before adopting the suggestion in the argument.

Argument Task 28

The following was written as a part of an application for a small-business loan by a group of developers in the city of Monroe.

"Jazz music is extremely popular in the city of Monroe: over 100,000 people attended Monroe's annual jazz festival last summer, and the highest-rated radio program in Monroe is 'Jazz Nightly,' which airs every weeknight. Also, a number of well-known jazz musicians own homes in Monroe. Nevertheless, the nearest jazz club is over an hour away. Given the popularity of jazz in Monroe and a recent nationwide study indicating that the typical jazz fan spends close to $1,000 per year on jazz entertainment, a jazz music club in Monroe would be tremendously profitable."

Write a response in which you examine the stated and/or unstated assumptions of the argument. Be sure to explain how the argument depends on these assumptions and what the implications are for the argument if the assumptions prove unwarranted.

NOTE: The above topic has wording similar to Agrument Task 27 of GRE Analytical Writing Solutions to the Real Essay Topics - Book 1. However, if you read carefully you will notice that the task instructions are different. Hence, it is very important to read the topic as well as its instructions completely before you start to write your response.

Strategies

A good place to start your analysis is by creating a statement that reveals the main idea of the argument. Although the writer is creating an argument, he may ultimately be stating a position, making a recommendation, or making a prediction. It may be helpful for you to determine which of these formats is most evident in the argument.

Based on attendance at last year's jazz festival in Monroe and the average amount of money that jazz fans spend on entertainment each year, a group of developers propose to build a jazz club in Monroe which is home to several jazz musicians.

Assumptions:

a) The attendance at the jazz festival indicates the genre's popularity in Monroe.

b) The jazz festival draws large crowds every year.

c) The jazz musicians perform regularly and would perform at a club in Monroe.

d) Jazz fans will spend an average of $1000 per year at a jazz club in Monroe.

e) Attendance at the jazz club will enable the owners to make a profit.

f) There are enough jazz fans to support two jazz clubs an hour away from each other.

Alternative explanations:

a) Last year's attendance at the jazz festival was much higher than normal.

b) Jazz musicians prefer to live in a town different from the one(s) in which they perform.

c) The jazz musicians in Monroe are retired.

d) Monroe's jazz club will need popular artists to encourage fans to spend $1000 per year.

e) A portion of the $1000 is spent on lodging and travelling rather than directly on jazz entertainment itself.

After completing these steps, you should have enough material to write your analysis. Remember that you are not creating a position of your own; you are evaluating the strengths and weaknesses of the existing argument. You do not have to include all of the points that you have created in your prewriting. In fact, during the process of drafting your analysis, other ideas may come to mind, and, if they strengthen your analysis, you should include them.

Sample Essay

A group of developers has made some assumptions about conditions in Monroe that seem to favor opening a jazz club there. Any lending institution will want to test those assumptions before laying out a considerable sum of money to renovate an existing structure or build a new one for the purpose of entertainment. The developers will need to show that their assumptions are based on verifiable facts.

These developers first assume that the attendance at last year's jazz festival in Monroe proves the popularity of the genre in this geographic location. The basis of this assumption holds true only if 100,000 attendees is a typical total. A number of factors may have contributed to what appears to be a high number. The performers at last year's festival may have larger fan bases than groups in previous years. Unless the festival organizers can continue to attract popular jazz acts, the attendance may revert to lower numbers. The organizers may have offered special ticket prices last year in an effort to attract a larger audience. They may have to do the same this year or subsequent years to obtain high numbers of attendees. Other jazz festivals may have been cancelled or may have seen reduced attendance due to poor weather, leaving jazz fans hungry for entertainment, which they found in Monroe. The popularity of jazz in Monroe can be supported by the festival attendance only if a large portion of Monroe's population attended the festival. It may be held in Monroe because the town has a superior venue.

Revealing that a number of well-known jazz musicians live in Monroe leads to the assumption that they will perform at the jazz club. Upon further scrutiny, lenders might discover that those jazz musicians are either retired or booked for most of the year in other locations. These musicians may consider Monroe as a place to get away from it all and have no desire to perform in their home town. Unless the developers can attract equally well-known and talented musicians to their club, they may find it difficult to be profitable.

Based on a survey revealing that the average jazz fan spends $1000 per year on jazz-related entertainment, the developers assume that jazz fans that live in or come to Monroe will also spend that amount every year. The truth about an average is that some fans spend more than $1000 per year and some spend less. The survey does not say that those fans spent that amount of money at jazz clubs. If the fans travel to visit clubs, a considerable portion of their spending could be for lodging, food, gas, or air fare. They may spend all or some of that money on recordings or music lessons. The Monroe club owners may have to provide a selection of jazz- related retail items to supplement the income from admission to the club.

The developers disclose that the closest jazz club is over an hour away to support the assumption that making jazz entertainment more convenient for the people in and around Monroe is a recipe for success. Before accepting this at face value, the lenders will need to know how many people live in the area. Monroe may be a small town, requiring the jazz club to draw attendees from a wide area. If traveling over an hour is an obstacle, the club in Monroe may suffer from a lack of nearby population. Regardless of distance, the other club may be very popular because of the quality of entertainment it offers, and the club in Monroe may not be able to equal its draw.

The lenders need more detailed information to prove or refute the assumptions inherent in the developers' argument. The risk inherent in any investment of this nature must be minimized before a bank or other investor opens its checkbook.

Argument Task 29

There is now evidence that the relaxed pace of life in small towns promotes better health and greater longevity than does the hectic pace of life in big cities. Businesses in the small town of Leeville report fewer days of sick leave taken by individual workers than do businesses in the nearby large city of Masonton. Furthermore, Leeville has only one physician for its one thousand residents, but in Masonton the proportion of physicians to residents is five times as high. Finally, the average age of Leeville residents is significantly higher than that of Masonton residents. These findings suggest that people seeking longer and healthier lives should consider moving to small communities.

Write a response in which you examine the stated and/or unstated assumptions of the argument. Be sure to explain how the argument depends on these assumptions and what the implications are for the argument if the assumptions prove unwarranted.

Strategies

A good place to start your analysis is by creating a statement that reveals the main idea of the argument. Although the writer is creating an argument, he may ultimately be stating a position, making a recommendation, or making a prediction. It may be helpful for you to determine which of these formats is most evident in the argument.

By comparing the small town of Leeville to the neighboring large city of Masonton, the author of this argument concludes that living in a small town promotes better health and longevity.

Assumptions:

a) Residents of smaller towns are healthier than residents of large cities.

b) Residents of small towns have less serious illnesses than those in large cities.

c) A relaxed pace of life is healthier than a hectic pace.

d) Small towns have a more relaxed pace of life than do large cities.

e) Workers call in sick only when they are genuinely ill.

f) One doctor is sufficient to treat the one thousand residents of Leeville.

Alternative explanations:

a) Leeville is a retirement community.

b) Masonton is home to more than one college.

c) Masonton has a large medical center.

d) People from Leeville seek medical treatment in Masonton.

e) Doctors may live in Masonton and work in other towns.

After completing these steps, you should have enough material to write your analysis. Remember that you are not creating a position of your own; you are evaluating the strengths and weaknesses of the existing argument. You do not have to include all of the points that you have created in your prewriting. In fact, during the process of drafting your analysis, other ideas may come to mind, and, if they strengthen your analysis, you should include them.

Sample Essay

The author of this argument uses the small town of Leeville and the large city of Masonton as examples of evidence that shows life in a small town is better for one's health than is life in a large city. The assumptions in the argument are based on some vague generalities without real numbers or statistics to clarify them. A number of alternatives can shoot holes in the substance of this position.

The argument assumes that people live longer in Leeville because it is a small town. It may simply be that older people have chosen to live in a small town rather than in the large city of Masonton. Anyone traveling up and down either coast of Florida, especially during the winter months, will pass through dozens of small towns where the average age is considerably higher than the average age in the cities of that state. In fact, those towns are largely populated by the elderly, at least for several months of the year. They are retirement communities. Senior citizens from colder states flock there each autumn and stay until late spring. Without facts to the contrary, one could assume that Leeville, also, is a retirement community. There may be covenants that prohibit people under a certain age, say 55, from living there. Residents of Leeville may not have selected this community because the pace of life is slower; they have, in fact, created that pace simply by living there. In contrast, large cities are bound to have a broader demographic and a lower average age as a result. The population will be a mix of young singles, families with young children, along with some senior citizens.

The higher proportion of doctors to residents in Masonton could arise from the presence of one or more medical centers in the city. In fact, it would be hard to name or imagine a large city without several health care facilities. Therefore, assuming that the larger number of doctors in Masonton derives from the greater number of sick people there may be erroneous. The elderly almost always require visits to a number of specialists, especially cardiologists, oncologists, and rheumatologists. A town of one thousand residents is not likely to have physicians practicing in those specialties. The one doctor in Leeville can probably provide sufficient care for minor ailments, but serious conditions must be treated in Masonton. Older citizens may prefer to live in smaller towns with a slower pace of life but desire comprehensive medical care to be in close proximity.

The assumption that Leeville's citizens are much older than the citizens of Masonton needs some further examination. The significant difference in median age between Leeville and Masonton may be a result of Masonton's having an unusually large percentage of young people. It would not be unreasonable to expect that Masonton has one or more colleges; most large cities do. When classes are in session, the average age of Masonton residents would drop considerably. One of these colleges may even have a medical school which contributes to the high number of doctors in the city.

Assuming that all small towns exhibit the same characteristics of Leeville is risky. Small towns in rural or remote areas may not provide a healthy lifestyle for their residents. People of all ages in these towns are likely to find quality health care difficult to access. Certainly, the residents will have to travel some distance to see specialists of any sort. In the case of an emergency, a citizen may have to wait a significant amount of time for help to arrive and spend additional time being transported to a medical facility. Heart attacks and strokes, common among the elderly, are survivable if treated quickly, something not likely to occur in small, rural towns.

The longevity of Leeville residents may be a direct result of its proximity to the large city of Masonton. A healthy life requires balance. Leeville residents can relax in the comfort of their homes in the quiet, small town but be stimulated by the activities available in Masonton. Remaining active and interested and living close to adequate healthcare is as good a recipe for longevity as residing in a small town where little ever happens.

Argument Task 30

The following appeared in a memo from the business manager of a chain of cheese stores located throughout the United States.

"For many years all the stores in our chain have stocked a wide variety of both domestic and imported cheeses. Last year, however, all of the five best-selling cheeses at our newest store were domestic cheddar cheeses from Wisconsin. Furthermore, a recent survey by Cheeses of the World magazine indicates an increasing preference for domestic cheeses among its subscribers. Since our company can reduce expenses by limiting inventory, the best way to improve profits in all of our stores is to discontinue stocking many of our varieties of imported cheese and concentrate primarily on domestic cheeses."

Write a response in which you examine the stated and/or unstated assumptions of the argument. Be sure to explain how the argument depends on these assumptions and what the implications are for the argument if the assumptions prove unwarranted.

Strategies

A good place to start your analysis is by creating a statement that reveals the main idea of the argument. Although the writer is creating an argument, he may ultimately be stating a position, making a recommendation, or making a prediction. It may be helpful for you to determine which of these formats is most evident in the argument.

The manager of the cheese store uses the results from a survey conducted by the magazine, Cheeses of the World, to recommend that his business discontinue stocking imported cheeses and focus on domestic cheeses in an effort to increase profits.

Assumptions:

a) Sales in the newest store predict what will be most popular in the chain's other stores.

b) The survey in Cheeses of the World applies to stores in every country.

c) The profit margin on imported and domestic cheeses is the same.

Alternative explanations:

a) The newest store is located in Wisconsin.

b) Best-selling cheeses are not necessarily the most profitable.

After completing these steps, you should have enough material to write your analysis. Remember that you are not creating a position of your own; you are evaluating the strengths and weaknesses of the existing argument. You do not have to include all of the points that you have created in your prewriting. In fact, during the process of drafting your analysis, other ideas may come to mind, and, if they strengthen your analysis, you should include them.

Sample Essay

It is the job of the business manager to take care of the bottom line. If he were able to increase profits, the owners of the business will be happy. In the case of this chain of cheese stores, the business manager may be putting the cart before the horse by suggesting that the stores focus on domestic cheeses only. While this argument seems logical on the surface, the stated and unstated assumptions in it deserve closer scrutiny before the company owners decide to jump on this wagon.

The readers of the memo may assume that the popularity of Wisconsin cheeses in the newest store predict similar success with domestic cheeses in their other stores. This may or may not be significant. If the newest store is located in Wisconsin, all bets are off. Customers of the store would be inclined to support their local cheese makers. Wisconsin is, after all, the Dairy State, and fans of the Green Bay Packers are known as Cheeseheads and wear foam hats that look like wedges of cheese when attending a Packers' game. If the company has a store in Vermont, a state replete with dairy farms, it likely sells more Vermont cheeses than imported cheeses. Stores located in the country's largest cities like New York, Chicago, or Los Angeles are likely to sell more imported cheeses to satisfy the more demanding palates of their citizens or to supplement the ethnic diets of their diverse populations. Eliminating imported cheeses from the inventories in these stores could have a deleterious effect on profits.

The assumption that sales of domestic cheese will lead to increased profits may have holes in it. Profit can be expressed as a percentage or a dollar amount. It is derived from the amount of markup on the items sold in a store and is affected by general expenses of operation. Let's assume that the cheese stores have a 100% markup on their cheeses. In other words, they double the wholesale price to arrive at the retail price for each cheese. If a pound of Wisconsin cheese wholesales for $5.00, it will retail for $10.00, and the store realizes a gross profit of $5.00. Now, if a pound of imported cheese costs $10.00, and the same 100% markup is applied, it will retail for $20.00 per pound and gross $10.00. It's easy to see that, in this case, the store must sell twice as much domestic cheese to make the same profit as on the imported cheese. The popularity of domestic cheeses guarantees neither higher total sales nor greater profits.

Using survey results to make important decisions requires careful consideration. A survey conducted by Cheeses of the World among its subscribers indicates a growing preference for domestic cheeses. It would be helpful to know how many subscribers there are and what percentage of them completed the survey. If this is an international publication, some respondents may have been referring to cheeses that Americans could only buy as imports. The business manager of the American cheese company in the argument needs this information before assuming that the survey results support his recommendation.

Most chain stores tailor their inventory to the location of each store. Macy's will not promote the same merchandise in Bangor, Maine that it does in Dallas, Texas. Bangor is a small city surrounded by even smaller towns and large rural areas. The population is largely working class. Dallas is home to millions, and the median income is far greater than that of Bangor residents. Macy's in Dallas is likely to have many more designer items than the Bangor store. This chain of cheese stores should probably adopt this same approach at each of its locations rather than assuming that the same items will sell well in each one. America is a country of great variety. Different ethnic, racial, and religious preferences exist side-by-side in communities across this great country. This cheese business should consider these variables before making decisions about the types of cheeses it stocks in each of its stores.

NOTES

45827772R00108

Made in the USA
Middletown, DE
14 July 2017